PREACHING The Parables

PREACHING

The Parables

JOHN R. BROKHOFF

Cycle B Texts
from Common, Lutheran,
and Roman Catholic
Lectionaries

C.S.S. Publishing Co., Inc.

Lima, Ohio

PREACHING THE PARABLES IN THE CYCLE B

Library of Congress Cataloging-in-Publication Data

Brokhoff, John R.
    Preaching the parables B.

    Bibliography: p.
    1. Jesus Christ — Parables — Study and teaching.
2. Preaching. 3. Common lectionary. 4. Lectionaries.
5. Bible. N.T. Gospels — Homiletical use. I. Title.
BT377.B76   1987   251   87-18261
ISBN 0-89536-880-3 (pbk.)

7866 / ISBN 0-89536-880-3
PRINTED IN U.S.A.

Table of Contents

Proper designations refer to the Common Lectionary
Pentecost designations refer to the Lutheran Lectionary
Ordinary Time designations refer to the Roman Catholic Lectionary.

Introduction

The current interest in narrative or story preaching has called attention to Jesus' parables, since many of the parables are stories. Is there a preacher — especially one who uses the Lectionary for preaching — who does not preach on a parable from time to time?

But how can we preach a parable most effectively? Should we simply tell the parable in our own words and let it stand on its own feet without any pulpit interpretation, explanation, or application? Should we allow people to understand the lesson of the parable for themselves? But even the Disciples often did not understand a parable, and had to ask Jesus for an explanation.

Or does a preacher more properly handle a parable by determining the main point, theme, or lesson taught by the parable, and then contructing a sermon on that theme? There may be no need in this case to consider the complicating details of a parable. The central theme becomes the springboard for a thematic sermon whether the theme be that of repentance, caring for the poor, or forgiveness.

Or does a preacher spiritualize or allegorize a parable in order to preach on it? Does each detail or character in the parable have a hidden meaning which must be explained by the preacher in order for the parable to have something to say about life today?

And then, of course, there is the possibility of treating a parable in an expository fashion. Not only the main theme but also the main points of the theme come from the parable. The Prodigal Son parable breaks down into three persons. The parable of the Sower lends itself to a fourfold type of listener.

These and other possibilities indicate that preaching about parables is not as easy as it looks. Each parable is different and calls for independent consideration. This book is offered as an aid to this necessary study in sermon preparation.

The Parables in Cycle B

The parables in Cycle B, are taken primarily from the Gospel of Mark. Nevertheless, Cycle B does not contain all of the parables in Mark. The Parable of the Sower, the Lamp under the Bowl, the Tenants in the Vineyard, and the parable concerning marriage in heaven may be considered in either Cycles A or C.

While Mark is used as the Gospel for Cycle B, the Gospel of John is used twenty Sundays in place of Mark. Four of these Sundays contain metaphorical tales which we may treat as parables. This is legitimate because a parable is often described as an extended metaphor. In Cycle B, then, we deal with the Good Shepherd, the True Vine, and Jesus, the Bread of Life (two Sundays).

The Four C's Format

In this book we will consider each parable according to four C's: context, content, contemplation, and contact.

1. Context: A parable is not an independent unit, but is related to a subject or problem which Jesus is handling at the time. It is important for us to fully define the setting of the parable, taking note of what precedes and follows it. The parable is also part of the Gospel lesson appointed for a certain Sunday in the church year. How, then, does the parable in the Gospel lesson relate to the theme of the day and to the other lessons? Finally we need to put the parable in the perspective of the entire Scriptures.

2. Content: What does the parable say or teach? What is the general theme and the most important point? Is there more than one idea being expressed? Who are the personnae in the parable, and what does each represent? To be certain that we understand the meaning of the parable, we need to translate it into our own words (precis). To further clarify the most important idea, we should summarize the truth of the parable in one sentence (thesis). Out of this thesis will then emerge a theme which will become the central point of the proposed sermon. More specifically, we should also note words or phrases that need to be examined closely and carefully defined. A theological wordbook would be helpful here.

3. Contemplation: Now that we see the parable in perspective and have a grasp of the message of the parable, t' ᵊ time for deeper reflection has come — for thought, listening, meditating, and prayer. How should we understand the parable? What does it mean to me and my people? What is the parable saying to us? Do you have any unique insights into the truth of the parable? Do you see any sermon possibilities?

4. Contact: The time for action has come. We must ask ourselves whether the subject of the parable has any relevance for today's society. Does the parable address a question that the people are asking? Is there a need in the church which this parable would help to fill? It is time, in other words, for the rubber to hit the road. The revelation of the parable must be made relevant to the people who will fill the pews this Sunday. What is its special relationship to them? What are their needs, their questions, and their problems? If you can find no point of significant contact, then it is better to forget the parable! To help make the sermon indigenous to life, illustrative materials are suggested.

What Others Say

After — and only *after* — going through this four C's process for yourself, you may want to know what others have to say about the particular parable you are using this Sunday. The following books may then be helpful:

Bailey, Kenneth — *Poet and Peasant.* Eerdmanns, 1976.
Buttrick, George — *The Parables of Jesus.* Harper, 1928.
Crossan, John — *In Parables.* Harper and Row, 1985.
Dodd, C. H. — *The Parables of the Kingdom.* Scribners, 1961.
Granskou, David — *Preaching on the Parables.* Fortress, 1972.
Hunter, Archibald — *Interpreting the Parables.* Westminster, 1960.
Jeremias, Joachim — *The Parables of Jesus.* Scribners, 1962.
Jones, G. V. — *The Art and Truth of the Parables,* 1964.
Linnemann, Eta — *Jesus of the Parables,* 1966.
Ogilvie, Lloyd — *Autobiography of God.* Regal, 1979.
Pentecost, J. D. — *The Parables of Jesus.* Zondervan, 1982.
Purdy, John — *Parables at Work.* Westminster, 1985.
Redding, David — *The Parables He Told.* Revell, 1962.
TeSelle, Sallie — *Speaking in Parables.* Fortress, 1975.
Via, Dan — *The Parables,* 1967

Preaching the Parables

In Mark we read that Jesus "did not speak to them without a parable" (Mark 4:34), while the Lectionary tells us that over a period of three years (Series A, B, and C) a preacher has forty-one opportunities to speak on a parable. In this period of time, preachers could preach on a parable almost every Sunday for a year and, as such, parables could constitute nearly one-third of a three-year program of preaching. Of course the parables could be avoided altogether if the sermons were based on a text selected from either the First or Second Lesson of the Lectionary.

Confronted with the many opportunities of preaching on the parables, a preacher faces questions such as these:

1. Is it sufficient to tell the parable in one's own words without providing any interpretation or application? Is it enough just to tell the story?

2. Is there more than one point to a parable?

3. Is it permissible to allegorize or spiritualize a parable?

4. How should one interpet and understand a parable? Jesus asks, "Do you not understand this parable?" (Mark 4:13)

5. How is a parable rightly used in a sermon?

Jesus' Use of Parables

If Jesus used parables in his teaching and preaching, then so can we. We can use our own parables. Or, better yet, we can preach on his parables. New Testament scholars agree that the parables are perhaps the most characteristic and most authentic of Jesus' teachings. Along with the Beatitudes and the Lord's Prayer, the parables are among the most familiar and deeply loved portions of the New Testament.

Jesus used many parables in his teaching and preaching. Parables constitute approximately one-third of his teachings, and their number lies somewhere between fifty and seventy. Matthew reports that Jesus "told them many things in parables," (Matthew 13:3) and goes even farther in writing that, "Indeed, he said *nothing* to them without a parable." (Matthew 13:34) If this is the case, then the reported number of seventy parables in the Gospels is actually but a tiny portion of the parables he gave.

Moreover, Jesus was content not merely to relate his parables, but he also took pains to explain them to his Disciples: "He did not speak to them without a parable, but privately to his own Disciples he explained everything." (Mark 4:34) According to Mark, then, Jesus told the parables to the public, but later explained the deeper meanings of the parables to those who were privileged to know the secret of the Kingdom. Referring to the parable of the sower and the seed, for example, Jesus asked his Disciples, "Do you not understand this parable?", and then proceeded to explain the significance of the tale. (Mark 4:13-20) We, however, could well ask today's preacher the same question that Philip asked the Ethiopian eunuch: "Do you understand what you are reading?" (Acts 8:30) How can we preach a parable if we do not understand it, and how can we understand the parable unless once again Jesus opens our minds to understand the Scriptures as he opened the minds of the two men on the road to Emmaus? (Luke 24:45)

Symphony of Similitudes

Many people have difficulty fully understanding an abstract truth of principle unless they are helped to see the truth as well as hear it. It is the preacher's task to put eyes into the ears of his audience so that they can say, "Now we *see* what you mean." To make the truth visible to all, we may use various literary devices called **similitudes.** The parable is one essential instrument in the symphony of similitudes:

1. Simile. A simile is the simplest form of similitude. It is a figure of speech which compares two unlike things in a phrase often introduced by "like" or "as." Example: "All we like sheep have gone astray." (Isaiah 53:6)

2. Analogy. In this case two or more things have a resemblance to each other. Example: When King Saul pursues David to kill him,

David asks why he wants to kill "a dead dog" or go "after a flea." (1 Samuel 24:14)

3. Metaphor. A word or phrase denoting one kind of object or idea is used in place of another to suggest a likeness between them. A metaphor is an extended simile. Example: "I am the good shepherd." (John 10:11)

4. Allegory. An allegory is a way of speaking figuratively. An allegory is a symbolic representation of truth — of an idea or moral or religious principle. Example: "The Lord is my shepherd." (Psalm 23:1) To say that the "Lord" is Jesus is to use allegory.

5. Parable. A parable is an extended metaphor in the form of a story. Examples: the Prodigal Son (Luke 15:11-32) or Nathan's story told to David (2 Samuel 12:1-6).

A parable is a major similitude which explains or describes some spiritual truth or principle. The Hebrew word for "parable" is "mashal," meaning "be like." The corresponding Greek word is "parabole," meaning the placing of one thing alongside another for comparison so that a parable is a kind of parallelism. A common contemporary definition of a parable says that it is an "earthly story with a heavenly meaning." This may be illustrated with the following diagram:

In a parable there may be parallels drawn between the earthly and the heavenly, the physical and the spiritual, the sacred and the secular, the timely and the timeless, and the concrete and the abstract. The principle, truth, or moral maxim is the common point of comparison. From the earthly story we may determine the underlying message. Certain parables may have a single dominating principle or truth to illustrate, while more allegorical forms may present us with many symbols to be interpreted. Writing in the

Christian Century (11/5/80) Walter Wink describes parables:

> *Parables are tiny lumps of coal squeezed into diamonds, condensed metaphors that catch the rays of something ultimate and glint it at our lives. Parables are not illustrations; they do not support, elaborate, or simplify a more basic idea. They are not ideas at all, nor can they ever be reduced to theological statements. They are the jeweled portals of another world; we cannot see through them like windows, but through their surfaces are refracted lights that would otherwise blind us — or pass unseen.*

The Story of the Church's Interpretation

1. Allegory is an ancient and popular method of interpreting the parables, and many examples of it can be found in the New Testament. According to Mark, for instance, the Disciples asked Jesus to explain the parable of the sower and the seed. (Mark 4:3-9) and in response Jesus used allegory in showing the seed that represents "the Word" while the different soils represent the different kinds of people who hear the Word. (Mark 4:14-20)

Paul also used allegory. In (Galatians 4:24) referring to the two wives of Abraham, Sarah and Hagar — one a free woman and the other a slave — Paul tells us explicitly that "this is an allegory." The two wives, said Paul, are the symbols of the two covenants of the Law on Mount Sinai and of the new Jerusalem.

Allegory was popularized by Origen (A.D. 185-254). It was his primary method of Biblical interpretation, and for centuries it was the chief method of interpretation for all. The great Saint Augustine, for example, used allegory in explaining the Good Samaritan. He found in the parable eighteen allegorical comparisons which included the following:

Parable		Allegory
1. "Certain man"	=	1. Adam
2. "Thieves"	=	2. The devil and his angels
3. "Half dead"	=	3. Half dead with sin
4. "Samaritan"	=	4. Jesus
5. "Oil"	=	5. Comfort of good hope

6. "Beast"	=	6. Flesh in which Jesus came
7. "Inn"	=	7. Church
8. "Morrow"	=	8. Resurrection
9. "Innkeeper"	=	9. Paul

Allegory is still being used today, but we must be careful not to misuse it as well. In the parable of the Prodigal Son, for example we may properly interpret the father as the "loving and patient heavenly Father," or we might consider the elder son to represent Israel and the younger son to be the sinful Gentiles. Improper use of allegory, on the other hand, can make the Scriptures appear to mean whatever we want them to mean. Preachers dealing with Apocalypticism or Eschatology, for example, are often guilty of such misguided allegorical interpretation in identifying a number or beast in the Bible as a contemporary person, nation, or event.

2. One Point. For 1900 years the church used allegory to understand the parables. Luther and Calvin used other interpretations as well, but 17th century Protestant Scholasticism returned to the use of allegory.

Adolf Julicher (1857-1938) was the person who broke the tradition of using allegory as the primary method of interpretaion. Julicher insisted that a parable had one main point — one truth, one principal — and the details in the parable were subordinate to and supportive of this single truth. Because of Julicher, the church was temporarily finished with using allegory as the method of interpreting the parables.

Julicher's position causes contemporary preachers to ask:

A. If it is true that a parable has only one point, how can we accurately determine what that point is?

In the parable of the Pharisee and Publican at prayer in the temple (Luke 18:9-14), for example, is the main point that of "humility" — e.g., "Who humbles himself will be exalted" — or is it "justification" — e.g., "This man went down to his house justified."?

B. Could there be more than one point in a parable?

Consider the parable of the Prodigal Son (Luke 15:11-32); are there not several major points to be considered? One important point, for example, is the repentance of the younger son, but there is also a wonderful illustrative point of a patient and loving father, i.e., certainly the elder son's attitude and spirit have something vital to say to those who stay "home" and are faithful.

3. Form Criticism. The leading Form Critics, Dibelius and Bultmann, disagreed with Julicher that a parable had only one point. Though by "form criticism" these scholars attempted to discover the intrinsic meaning of a parable by examining the parable in the context of its orignial setting. They held that many interpretations of the parables were the product of the early church and its circumstances rather than representing the original teaching of Jesus. Form critics argued that we must consider three different levels in examining a parable:

A. The original words of Jesus.
B. The adaptation of the parable by the church to contemporary conditions. For example, form critics argued that the popular explanation of the parable of the Sower (Mark 4:14-20) was a result of the early church shaping a response to a situation in which preaching of the Word was not being universally accepted.
C. The biased interpretation of the evangelist-writer. Form critics point to Mark 4:11-12 as a clear example. Here Jesus is reported as saying that he spoke in parables in order to hide the truth from the people and to share the truth only with the Disciples. This seems to contradict Jesus' avowed purpose in wanting *all* to know the truth so that they might be forgiven. Most form critics argue that Mark added these verses to explain why contemporary Jews rejected the preachings of the Apostles.

4. The Eschatological Dimension. C. H. Dodd (1935) and Joachim Jeremias (1947) added the eschatological dimension to the interpretation of parables. They held that the parables are to be understood in the light of the new age inaugurated by Christ. The parables are unique products of the Kingdom and, as a result, a moralistic interpretation was declared to be out of order. These outstanding scholars sought to recreate the original circumstances of the parable through a historical-critical method of biblical interpretation.

5. The Existential Perspective. In the 1970s, Dan Via criticized the historical-critical approach of Dodd, Jeremias, and Bultmann. Via claimed that the esthetic and human elements of the parables were being ignored, and held that because we cannot be certain of the original setting of the parables, the purpose of the parables ought to been seen as the providing of a better understanding of human existence. The language of the parables should be translated so that the text would become an event meaningful to a contemporary audience. Via looked upon the parables as esthetic objects aiding in the understanding of human existence, and in the exploration of human identity.

Our Dealing with the Parables

What can the contemporary preacher learn from the history of parable interpretation?

1. Through historical-critical analysis, we should attempt to detail the original setting and circumstances of the parable. Did the parable come directly from Jesus, or did the church or specific interpreter change or add to the parable?

2. By reading the parable several times, and then carefully reflecting upon it, we ought to determine the main truth or principle, of the parable. This might then become the thesis or theme of our sermon.

3. We should make certain that the details of the parable remain subordinate to the major point and are not emphasized out of proportion to their importance.

4. We should avoid spiritualizing or allegorizing the parable. The parable itself ought to be the vehicle to carry the truth.

5. An attempt should be made to give the parable a contemporary message by relating and applying the parable to everyday life.

Characteristics of Parables

Preachers should understand the common characteristics of

parables as a prerequisite to beginning deeper interpretation.

1. Parables are usually basic, brief, and beautiful. They deal with basic issues of life: humility, patience, persistence, compassion, repentance, watchfulness, and the like.

They are usually very brief. Parables are direct and to the point.

They are beautiful. Parables exhibit a supreme literary quality. Can the parables of the Good Samaritan, the Lost Sheep, and the Prodigal Son, for example, ever be surpassed in their simple poetry?

2. Parables are intended for the common people. The parables are directed to ordinary people and are about their lives. They address those who pound the streets, who labor long hours, who have burdens to bear. They are not to be restricted to scholars, or the intelligentsia, or the leisure class. The parables tell of everyday objects, common experiences, and familiar life situations. A parable may contain a robbery, a person aroused from sleep at midnight, people at prayer, and so forth.

3. Parables make us think. Listeners or readers are asked to come to their own conclusions or to provide answers to their questions. Parables use the case study method of teaching, and demand active inductive thought. They provide the situation, problem, or question and then provoke a reaction. Jesus used this inductive method many times: he once asked a lawyer, for example, "How do you read?", (Luke 10:26) and thereby answered a question *with* a question. Jesus makes us think so that we will come to an answer or conclusion on our own, and this is also a good technique for a sermon.

4. Parables use indirect communication. Parables present the gospel message in a manner which is persuasive but not dogmatic. The underlying principle is attractively clothed in a setting, a story, or an experience, and we may therefore receive the message in an indirect way which is more acceptable and palatable than a crudely direct mode of presentation. When Nathan told David the story of the rich man taking the poor man's only pet lamb, for example, David understood how the story applied to his own life ("I have sinned . . .") without undue prodding or persuasion. Nathan's message was more meaningful because it was more subtle than an explicit admonition.

5. Parables call for a decision. In the Good Samaritan story, Jesus says to the lawyer, "Go and do thou likewise." Parables are not primarily for entertainment, but are means of confronting us with the necessity for a decision or response.

6. Parables explain. The parables are not intended to hide the truth or to confuse us. They are supposed to enable common people to know and understand the truth about God, life, and themselves. The parables throw light on dark subjects, and relieve ignorance and misunderstanding. Parables should enable each of us to say, "Now I see what you mean."

Advent 1

1. The Doorkeeper

Mark 13:32-37

[32] *"But of that day or that hour no one knows, not even the angels in heaven nor the Son, but only the Father.* [33] *Take heed, watch; for you do not know when the time will come.* [34] *It is like a man going on a journey, when he leaves home and puts his servants in charge, each with his work, and commands the doorkeeper to be on the watch.* [35] *Watch therefore — for you do not know when the master of the house will come, in the evening, or at midnight, or at cockcrow, or in the morning —* [36] *lest he come suddenly and find you asleep.* [37] *And what I say to you I say to all: Watch."*

Context

Context of Advent 1 in the Church Year

In Series A, B, and C the first Sunday in Advent is Parousia Sunday. Advent is the first season of the church year and, is therefore, the opening of a new church year. It is a season of preparation through repentance for the coming of Christ on Christmas. The church year deals with the Parousia on the first Sunday of the new church year and Eschatology at the end of the year. This can be seen in Series B. Advent 1 deals with the return of Christ (Mark 13:32-37) and Pentecost 26 (Proper 28) deals with the signs of the end of the world (Mark 13:24-32). The connecting link is verse 32 which is the opening verse of Advent 1 and the closing verse of Pentecost 26.

The theme of Advent 1 is the return of Christ at the end of time. The pericopes for the day and the propers deal with this theme. The Psalm sings: "Stir up thy might and come to save us." (Psalm 80:2) The Prayer of the Day pleads: "Stir up your power, O Lord, and come . . . " The Hymn of the Day begins, "Fling Wide the Door."

The Advent color of the paraments is either violet for repentance or blue for hope. The Advent wreath with one violet candle burning is in the chancel. It is appropriately lighted either at the beginning or end of the First Lesson.

At Christmas we celebrate the birth of Christ in 4 B.C. On Advent 1 on the other hand, we are happily anticipating and praying for Christ to come to our world today.

Context of the Lectionary

The three Lessons in the Lectionary are Advent 1-B relate to the theme of the Second Coming of Christ.

The First Lesson. (Isaiah 63:16—64:8) The newly-returned Babylonian exiles appeal to Yahweh to come to them in their nation's desolation and sin in order to help and save them. They base their appeal not on their worthiness to be helped but on the simple fact that Yahweh is their Father. Here we see a people lost in darkness, desolation, and despair lamenting their sins and crying to God to come to them and save them.

The Second Lesson. (1 Corinthians 1:3-9) While the Corinthian Christians wait for Jesus' return, they are assured that Christ will sustain them and free them from their sins when he appears on the last day.

Gospel. (Mark 13:32-37) Jesus says that he will return suddenly and unexpectedly just as a master may return from his journey at any time. In view of this, therefore, his disciples are instructed to watch, be awake, and work.

Context of the Gospel Lesson in Mark

The Gospel Lesson (Mark 13:32-37) is the closing portion of chapter 13 and is known as "The Little Apocalypse." In this chapter Jesus tells four Disciples the last things which will take place on earth at the time of his return: destruction of the temple, natural disasters, the persecution of God's people, the appearance of false messiahs, certain signs immediately preceding the end, and the parable of the fig tree.

It is important for the preacher to note that the parable of the fig tree will come in Proper 28 (see Chapter 8). In preaching on Advent 1, therefore, this aspect of the Parousia should be avoided so that there will not be duplication or repetition. If it is preached, however, the repetition will still be reduced in effect since the fig tree parable comes almost at the end of the church year.

Context of the Parable in the Pericope

The parable of the doorkeeper cannot be understood apart from the context of the pericope. Jesus is teaching his Disciples that no one except his Father knows when the end of the world will come and when he will return. It is, he says, like an owner or master of an estate who goes on a long trip without saying when he will return but only that it will be sudden and unexpected. Consequently, the servants need to fulfill their assigned tasks, stay awake, and watch for his return. The question at hand, therefore, is the time of his return and of the end of the cosmos. Since no one but God himself knows that time, the parable tells us, we must remain vigilantly ready and alert at *all* times. Jesus warns all of us to "Watch!"

Content

Precis of the Pericope: (Mark 13:32-37)

No one knows, not the angels nor even Jesus, the Son of God, the day or hour when the end of the world will occur and when Jesus will return. Only God the Father knows the time. Therefore, we are to take heed and watch because we do not know the time of the end. It is like a man going on a trip. When he leaves, he assigns work to his employees and commands the guard at the gate to be on the watch for his return. Likewise, we should watch, for Christ, like the master, will return at an unknown hour — in the evening, at midnight, or in the early morning. If we do not watch, the master will find us asleep. Jesus warns one and all: Watch!

Key Words in the Parable

1. "Only" (v. 32) *Only* God knows when the end of the world will come and when Jesus will return to judge the nations, and gather his people for life eternal. If even Jesus and the angels do not know the hour and day, of his return, then how could any human presume to possess this information? Yet in the first century some actually claimed they did have this information, but Jesus warned his Disciples not to pay attention to anyone who claimed such knowledge. Even Paul had some in his congregations who held that Jesus had already come, and through the centuries religious fanatics in many times have announced the day of Jesus' return, only to be proven wrong. If, after all, God the Father did not reveal the date to his Son, why would he disclose the secret to a sinful human being? The fact that we do not know the date of his return is precisely what gave Jesus the occasion to tell the parable of the doorkeeper.

2. **"Journey"** (v. 34) The master of the estate leaves on a trip, but where he is going and how long he will be gone is unknown. This is analogous to Jesus, the Master, because at his Ascension he took a journey to his Father's right hand in heaven, but we do not know when he will return to earth. This is why we must be ready at any hour to receive him.

3. **"Servants"** (v. 34) We Christians are to be like the "servants" of the master in the parable. When Jesus ascended, he gave the mission of reconciling the world to God to his servants. As the master in the parable asked his servants to work in his absence, so each Christian has been given his or her work of Kingdom extension by our Master. When Jesus returns, he will expect to find us working at our jobs, and we will be held accountable to him. In this sense, therefore, there is a judgment for Christians and non-Christians alike. We have a great deal of important work to do. We are not here to dream, to play, or to sleep because we are "in charge" (v. 34) of God's work in the world, and we thus have a tremendous responsibility.

4. **"Doorkeeper"** (v. 34) The doorkeeper was commanded to watch for the master's unexpected return. While the other servants are busy with their assigned tasks, the job of the doorkeeper is to announce the return of the owner. While we servants today are busy with our God-given tasks, who will tell us Christ is coming? It is for this reason that the church has its clergy and lay leaders. Preachers, teachers, lay professionals, administrators, and all the other leaders are today's watchmen on the Kingdom's towers. They

are set apart to be on the alert, to watch, and to announce the Master's coming. Nevertheless, *every* Christian is to be on the alert, for what Jesus said to a few Disciples he meant for all: "Watch!"

5. "Suddenly" (v.36) This is a key word which provides us with the reason for taking heed and watching. Not only will Christ come at an unknown hour, but he will also come suddenly. This unexpected and sudden arrival will not allow time for us to prepare for his coming at the last minute. There will be no opportunity to set our house in order or to suddenly get busy about our assigned tasks. We must, therefore, live each day as though it were our last — we must go about our tasks, live lives worthy of our calling, and seek to be in a state of grace at all times.

Contemplation

Before preaching on the Second Coming, a preacher faces certain questions and problems related to it. These need to be carefully considered before sermon preparation begins. It is a time of contemplation, in other words, following study of the context and the content of the parable.

Questions for Contemplation

Question 1 — Is Jesus really coming back to earth? If we do not believe in the Parousia, then how can we preach it? And neither do all of our people believe in Jesus' return. A 1986 survey by the Princeton Research Center reports that 62% of the American people believe Jesus will return. A preacher thus faces a significant portion of his/her people with little faith in the Parousia. How should we try to convince them?

There are also sincere Christians who believe that Jesus has already returned, arguing that Christ's Resurrection is spiritual rather than physical. They claim that Jesus came again on Easter when he returned from the dead, for example, while others feel that Jesus returned in the reception of the Holy Spirit, for the spirit of Christ is the Holy Spirit. (2 Corinthians 3:17) Furthermore, the church itself may be seen as the body of Christ, or as the contemporary incarnation of Christ. In his church, after all, he is present in Word and Sacraments.

Is Christ coming at the end of the world or is he not? If he is not, there certainly is no need for preaching on the Second Coming. But the Scriptures tell us that Christ will return: The Second Coming is mentioned 318 times in the New Testament and seven out of every ten chapters in the New Testament refer to the Parousia.

Moreover, the Christian church believes and teaches that Jesus is coming again. Throughout the centuries, the church has professed its faith in the ecumenical creeds, the Apostles and Nicene ("He will come again to judge the living and the dead.") and in the words of Paul, the church forever prays: "Maranatha — Our Lord, Come." (1 Corinthians 16:22)

If religious appeals are insufficient to convince us, we can make a more basic appeal to common sense. If Jesus does not return, then history will have no meaning or destiny and we must accept the Greek conception that history constantly repeats itself. But history for Christians is not cyclical but linear; history has a destination. History is *His story,* and reason therefore demands that there be a consummation of history. Justice requires evil to be vanquished and that truth, goodness, and love shall triumph. Christ needs to come to gather the living and the dead for their eternal home in heaven. The world as it exists today in its sin and injustice clearly cannot go on forever — not as long as God is in his heaven! Reason insists that there must be an end, a climax of history when God, through Christ, will end our story in victory.

Question 2 — In whose hands is the fate of the world? In the threatening light of nuclear arms, will there still be an earth to which Jesus will come? Will God's will be frustrated by the destructive power of humanity? This is not an idle question because humanity now has the power to destroy the human race. A Canadian physicist, Allen Munn, says that with the nuclear devices now in existence we "might cause the world and all in it to disintegrate in less than a minute." The world's nations now have 50,000 nuclear bombs — enough to destroy every major city in the world. And such a war would also result in a nuclear winter caused by a radioactive cloud that would hide the sun and lead to a worldwide famine. The radioactive blasts would contaminate the remaining water, food, and milk, and make human habitation impossible. Because of the increasing prospect of nuclear war, the Academy of Atomic Scientists has set its Doomsday clock at seven minutes before midnight.

Since human destruction of the earth would be counter to God's plan for Jesus' return, it should arouse and inspire all Christians to demand nuclear disarmament by all nations and to work for peace on earth. Maybe this alone is reason enough to preach on the Second Coming.

Question 3 — Why is the Second Coming left largely to sectarian churches? Why do the mainline churches neglect and/or ignore the Parousia while the Sectarians make it the primary subject for preaching and teaching? Following the Lectionary and the Church Year, mainline churches often only consider Christ's return once or twice a year, while Pentecostals, Charismatics, and Fundamentalists deal with it almost every Sunday.

Both extremes need to be avoided. The doctrine of the Second Coming should be kept in balance with the other doctrines of the Bible. Through the Church Year and Lectionary, the church keeps the Second Coming in proper perspective by designating the beginning and the end of the Church Year for the consideration of the Parousia. To ignore the Second Coming may prevent a congregation from understanding the important truth of the Parousia and its meaning for life today.

Permanent Preaching Values of the Parable

1. What do we know about Christ's return? Preceding the parable of the Doorkeeper, Jesus tells us that neither he nor the angels knows the time of his return. But there is much that we *do* know:

A. *The uncertainty of his coming* — the parable promises that the master is going to return at an unknown date. We know that he is coming. This fact has important implications for our lives:

History has a purpose.

Evil will be judged and destroyed — Justice will be done.

Victory for God and his Kingdom will be accomplished.

B. *The certainty of his coming.* Because we cannot know the hour, we are admonished to:

Wait patiently (Waiters) — v. 33

Work faithfully (Workers) — v. 34

Watch carefully (Watchers) v. 37

2. Work while you wait. When the master leaves on a trip, he "puts his servants in charge, each with his work." What shall we do while we wait for Christ's return? Should we be idle as some were in Paul's day? Eat, drink, and be merry? Separate ourselves from society? Through this parable, Jesus teaches us to work at our assigned tasks. (v. 34) This involves:

> Our use of talents
> Our responsibilities to serve
> Our eventual accountablity when Jesus returns

3. Jesus Watchers. Today many people are concerned with excess weight, and some even go so far as to join the "Weight Watchers" program. These people watch their weight very carefully. The parable of "The Doorkeeper" asks us only to pay a similiar degree of close attention to something far more important, and cautions that the opposite of "watching" is "sleeping." (v. 36) When we sleep, we are unconcerned and apathetic. To watch, therefore, means to be awake to what is happening. Christians are to watch:

> For the signs of the end.
> For the coming of Christ.

4. Life until he comes. The parable emphasizes the unexpected and sudden nature of Jesus' return. This means that last-minute preparations cannot be made, and therefore for readiness each day of our lives. What manner of lives should we live until Christ comes again? We must:

> Discharge our obligations ("Put his servants in charge")
> Perform our tasks ("Each with his work")
> Watch for Christ's return ("Commands the doorkeeper to be on the watch")

Contact

The parable's teaching must become relevant and immediately applicable to every person's daily life. So preachers must ask themselves, "How does the Parousia relate to my people? Are they interested in it and if not, how can they be interested? What difference should the sudden and unexpected return of Christ make in the life of a 20th-century person?"

Preachers first need to face the fact that approximately one-third of all Americans do not believe Jesus will ever return, and that probably a majority of those remaining are deeply apathetic. This constitutes a significant challenge to the preacher in making the Parousia real and vital for the average person's life. The subject matter and the approach used will have to be fashioned to confront this difficult set of circumstances.

Illustrative Materials

1. Jesus coming soon? Commuters on Conrail's New Haven line saw a billboard alongside the railroad that read: "The Lord is coming soon." Someone had written underneath: "Not if he takes the New Haven!"

2. Work while waiting. When an eclipse of the sun occured during a meeting of the Continental Congress, some of the legislators became alarmed and said fearfully, "It is the end of the world." Benjamin Franklin called for order and said, "It is either the end of the world or it is not. If it is, we should be faithful to our task. Light a candle and let us be about our business."

3. Watch. On April 12, 1912 the Titanic left Southampton for New York City or her maiden voyage with 2200 passengers on board. The new ship was as tall as an eleven-story building, 900 feet long, and weighed 46,000 tons. She was also considered to be a perfect ship, the best ever built. A crewman boasted, "God himself could not sink this ship." The ship sailed speedily and carelessly ahead among icebergs in the North Atlantic. When the Titanic struck an iceberg and sent out an SOS, another ship, the "Californian," was only ten miles away but failed to come to the rescue because the radio operator was *asleep.* As a result, 1100 lives were lost.

4. When the Master returns. Some years ago, a tourist visited a castle along Lake Como in Italy. A friendly old gardener opened the gates and showed him the gardens. The tourist asked the gardener, "When was your master last here?", and the old man answered, "Twelve years ago." "Does the master ever come?" "Never," replied the gardener. "But you keep the garden in such fine condition, just as though you expected your master to come tomorrow." The old man replied hastily, "Today, sir, today."

---

2. The Good Shepherd

John 10:11-18

---

[11]*"I am the good shepherd. The good shepherd lays down his life for the sheep.* [12]*He who is a hireling and not a shepherd, whose own the sheep are not, sees the wolf coming and leaves the sheep and flees; and the wolf snatches them and scatters them.* [13]*He flees because he is a hireling and cares nothing for the sheep.* [14]*I am the good shepherd; I know my own and my own know me,* [15]*as the Father knows me and I know the Father; and I lay down my life for the sheep.* [16]*And I have other sheep, that are not of this fold; I must bring them also, and they will heed my voice. So there shall be one flock, one shepherd.* [17]*For this reason the Father loves me, because I lay down my life, that I may take it again.* [18]*No one takes it from me, but I lay it down of my own accord. I have power to lay it down, and I have power to take it again; this charge I have received from my Father."*

John 10 is generally considered the "Good Shepherd" chapter in a manner similiar to the way that Hebrews 11 is often called the "faith" chapter. Jesus as the Good Shepherd has long been a popular concept. Even before the era of contemporary church architecture, for example, many churches had a large and prominent stained glass window depicting Jesus as the Good Shepherd holding in his arms a recovered sheep and leading a flock. This figure of Jesus as the Good Shepherd was also often found on the walls of the catacombs, where Jesus is usually shown carrying a sheep on his shoulders. The spiritual leader of a congregation is called a "pastor," of course, and this is the Latin word for "shepherd." And the most popular psalm through the centuries begins, "The Lord is my shepherd." Yet this popularity makes preaching on the concept very difficult. Because it is so well known, and has been preached so frequently, a preacher is often challenged to say something new or different about it.

Is the Good Shepherd account a parable? Some consider it to be more accurately termed as a metaphor. Most books about the parables do not define it as a parable and, indeed, John 10:6 is translated in different ways which makes clear definition difficult. The Revised Standard Version refers to a *"figure* Jesus used with them . . . "*, while the New King James Version says: "Jesus used this *illustration* . . ." Other versions of the bible, however, do refer to it as a parable. The Good News Bible, for example, headlines this section as "The *Parable* of the Shepherd," while the Good News Bible, King James Version, and New English Bible all use the word "parable" in verse 6. While it remains unclear whether or not "The Good Shepherd" is a parable in the strictest sense, we can nevertheless treat it more broadly as a similitude which embodies an important message in Jesus' teachings.

Context

Context of the Season

The parable of the Good Shepherd is presented in the Gospel for the fourth Sunday of Easter. This may seem strange until we consider the relationship between the parable and the Easter Season as a whole. In the post-Vatican II lectionary, Easter was expanded from a single day to an entire season. Before this time, we celebrated the resurrection on Easter Day, while the each Sunday following was called "Sunday *after* Easter." Since we now celebrate Easter for seven Sundays in the Easter Season, we refer to each Sunday as a "Sunday *of* Easter."

Easter 4 begins a new segment of readings in the Easter Gospels. On previous Sundays we have learned of the empty tomb (Easter 1), of how Jesus convinced Thomas that He has risen (Easter 2), and of Lukes's account in Easter 3 of Jesus' appearance to the assembled Disciples. Now Easter 4 arrives and brings the parable of the Good Shepherd.

Context of the Day

In the Church Year this Sunday has been known for many years as "Good Shepherd Sunday" or "Misericordia Domini." The Theme of the Day is "The Good Shepherd Lives," and the Psalm is the appropriately titled Psalm 23:1 "The Lord is my shepherd." The Prayer of the Day refers to Jesus as "the great shepherd of the sheep" and asks God the Father to "send us as shepherds . . ." The recommended Hymn of the Day is "The Lord's my Shepherd; I'll not Want." If the organ selections and the choir offerings are all on the same theme, then the worshipers will hear about the Good Shepherd from prelude to postlude. It is only proper, therefore, that the sermon should also deal with the Good Shepherd.

Context of the Lectionary

The three Lessons are also on the theme of the shepherd and the sheep.

The First Lesson. (Acts 4:8-12) After Peter and John heal a lame man at the beautiful gate of the temple, they are arrested and ordered the next day to explain how they performed the miracle. Peter explains that it was made possible in the name of Jesus whom they crucified and whom God raised from the dead.

The Second Lesson. (1 John 3:18-24) John calls attention to the comforting knowledge possessed by Christ's followers. Christians know they are of the truth, and they know that God lives in them because they have the Spirit. This corresponds to the Gospel section in which Jesus says he knows his sheep and his sheep know him.

Gospel. (John 10:11-18) Jesus is the Good Shepherd who, for the sake of his sheep, lays down his life and takes it up again. We should see the parable in the context of the whole chapter:

vv. 1-10 — Jesus says he is the door of the sheep.
vv. 11-18 — Jesus says he is the good shepherd.
vv. 19-21 — There is a divided reaction to Jesus' claims.
vv. 22-29 — Jesus attends the Feast of the Dedication where his life is threatened because he claims oneness with God.
vv. 40-42 — Jesus retires to the region of the Jordan.

Content

Precis: (John 10:11-18)

Jesus says: "I am the good shepherd. I am the good shepherd because a good shepherd dies for his sheep. A hired hand, who does not own the sheep, abandons the sheep when a wolf comes to snatch and scatter them. He runs away because he does not care for the sheep. I am the good shepherd who knows his sheep and whose sheep know him, just as the Father knows me and I know the Father. I lay down my life for the sheep. I have other sheep and I must gather them also. They will obey my voice. Then there will be one flock and one shepherd. My Father loves me because I sacrifice my life in order to get it back again. No one takes my life; I give it willingly. I have the power to give it and to resurrect it. I do this in obedience to God's orders."

Thesis: Jesus is the Good Shepherd because he cared enough to die for us and to rise again.

Theme: Jesus rose from the dead to be our Good Shepherd.

Key Words in the Parable

1. "Am" (v. 11) At the time Jesus actually said "I am," the present tense of the verb was appropriate. After almost 2000 years however, should it not be "I *was* the good shepherd"? The answer is to be found in what he said later in reference to his resurrection: "I have power to take it again." It is for this reason that this pericope of the good shepherd is appropriate for the season when the church celebrates Easter — i.e., by virtue of the resurrection, Jesus is a Shepherd for all times. The author of Hebrews for example, acknowledged this when he said that "Jesus Christ is the same yesterday and today and forever." (Hebrews 13:8) The last book of the Bible has Jesus saying: "I am the first and the last, and the living one; I died, and behold I am alive for evermore." (Revelation 1:17-18). Jesus, therefore, can say "I *am* the good shepherd" to us today just as surely as he did long ago to his followers in Palestine.

2. "The" (v. 11) Jesus does not say, "I am *a* good shepherd," but that "I am *the* good shepherd." This article is a key word because Jesus thereby sets forth his claim that he is the one and only shepherd of all peoples. Later he reaffirms his special role in declaring that "There shall be one flock, one shepherd." And in today's First Lesson, Peter affirms this when he states, "There is no other name under heaven given among men by which we must saved." (Acts 4:12). In the context of today's pluralistic society which believes that all roads lead to God, this claim of Jesus may seem arrogant and unduly exclusive. Nevertheless, it is the truth!

3. "Good" (v. 11) In the Greek language there are two words for "good." "Agathos" refers to a quality of morality, while "Kalos," the word in our text means "good" not only in the ethical sense but also in terms of love, sympathy, and concern. Jesus is the "good" shepherd, therefore, because he cares for his sheep. In contrast, the bad shepherd runs away in a time of danger and does not care if beasts kill and scatter the sheep. Because there is none good but God, Jesus is good because he is godly. And he is godly because he is the Son of a good God!

4. "Shepherd" (v. 11) The rough and rocky terrain of Israel lent itself to the raising of sheep and consequently, the shepherd was no doubt a familiar figure. The ancient shepherd lived with his sheep, and he was never off duty. Because he cared deeply for his sheep, he led them, provided for them, protected them from predators and poachers, and died for them when necessary. He probably knew them each by name, and certainly they knew the sound of his voice. We easily understand, therefore, why the figure of a shepherd was very popular in speaking of God and his appointed leaders.

God himself was often called a shepherd: "Give ear, O Shepherd of Israel . . ." (Psalm 80:1); "He shall feed his flock like a shepherd . . ." (Isaiah 40:11)

The leaders of the nation, including kings, priests, and prophets, were also frequently called shepherds. David was known as the "shepherd of Israel," while both Jeremiah and Ezekiel preached against the false shepherds of their day who fed themselves but not the sheep and who even could be said to scatter the sheep.

It was only natural then that Jesus used the same figure to identify himself. As a good shepherd he seeks the lost sheep, (Luke 15:3-7) and the newly-risen Jesus tells Peter to "feed his sheep" in order to prove his love.

From the very beginning, therefore, the church has continued to use the title "shepherd" for church leaders. When Paul leaves Ephesus for Jerusalem for the last time, to cite another example, he refers to the church as "the flock" and urges the elders to feed the sheep. Peter later commands the elders: "Tend the flock of God . . ." (1 Peter 5:2) And in our day, of course, the spiritual leader of a congregation is usually called the pastor (shepherd).

5. "Sheep" (v. 11) If Jesus is the shepherd, then his followers are his "sheep." A lost person is termed a lost sheep, and Jesus had compassion for a crowd of non-believers because they were like sheep without a shepherd. Psalm 95 says it nicely: "He is our God, and we are the people of his pasture and the sheep of his hand."

And indeed, people are much like sheep. We gather into crowds, and often blindly follow a leader. Like sheep, we are also gullible and may stand in line even when we do not know why. Our slogan so often seems to be "Everybody's doing it; why shouldn't I?" We therefore eagerly embrace fads, fashions, and trends without asking the reason or sense. We are shortsighted, again like sheep, for it is said that sheep can see no farther than six feet in front of them. Moreover, sheep are largely defenseless — a dog bites, a cat scratches, a porcupine has quills, a skunk has odor, but a sheep has little to protect itself. It is an easy prey.

Contemplation

Because parables constitute a literary form in which meanings are not explicit, readers, listeners, and especially preachers must invest much time and reflection to understand the meaning. We are no different from the Disciples in this regard for they also had difficulty understanding Jesus' parables. We are at the point of our study of the Good Shepherd at which we must try to ascertain the spiritual and theological message.

Questions for Contemplation

1. Why was the parable of the Good Shepherd chosen as a Gospel for the Easter season? On the surface, this parable seems to have no reference or connection with the Resurrection being celebrated during the Easter season. That God the Son knows us, guides us, gathers us, provides for us, protects us, and dies for us can be preached and appreciated at any time of the year. Is this parable therefore misplaced? I think not. During the Easter season, when we focus on the Resurrection, we should also see that the Good Shepherd did not only die for his sheep but that he also rose again by his power. Without the Resurrection, therefore, Jesus would have been a good shepherd for his generation but not for those following. But Christ is today's Good Shepherd who lives and reigns to eternity, and who is alive, for example, to care for his sheep in the First Lesson when a cripple is healed through the power of Jesus' name. (Acts 4:8-12)

2. What is the main idea behind the figure of the Good Shepherd? The focus of the parable is not on false shepherds (hirelings), or on the sheep. It is rather, on the shepherd himself. It tells us about the nature of God's Son, and it answers the question, "What kind of a God do we have?" We have a shepherd, a pastor; we could call him "Pastor Jesus." And what kind of a pastor is he? There is none other like him, for in Jesus we know that we have a God who knows us, cares for us, protects us, and provides for us. And the specially wonderful aspect of our shepherd is that this pastor rose from the dead and lives forever to "pastor" us. This is the good news we preach on this Good Shepherd Sunday.

3. Is the metaphor of "The Good Shepherd" still relevant? The figure of shepherd and sheep was appropriate in Jesus' day because Christ lived in a pastoral and agricultural society. Most people knew the characteristics and work of a shepherd, and sheep were as common then as dogs and cats are to us today. Have any of us, on the other hand, ever met a shepherd? How many of us have even seen a real sheep other than in a picture, movie or zoo? This concept is probably foreign to most inhabitants of an industrial and technological society. This presents a challenge to a preacher to make the metaphor of Christ as "The Good Shepherd" speak to this generation. Can we think of a more familiar figure than a shepherd to convey similar qualities? Since this is not likely, the preacher must point beyond the surface concept of a shepherd to the deeper truths a shepherd once expressed.

4. Are we all shepherds or are we sheep? When we attempt to apply the parable to the church today, should we deal with the members of the congregation as shepherds or sheep? Should we preach to convince people to be good shepherds? In recent years the emphasis in the church has been on the concept of the priesthood of all believers, so that every member is seen as a minister. A church leader recently wrote, for example, "It could speak to hearts warmed of a newly grasped concept as old as the gospel itself, the idea that we are *all* ministers." If we are *all* ministers (shepherds and pastors), then where are the sheep? Perhaps the "priesthood of all believers" errs in placing too great an emphasis upon the number of shepherds at the expense of a more important concern with quality and commitment. According to the New Testament, the people of the church are the sheep that are led by pastors (shepherds). Jesus is our one great shepherd, and the called, ordained leaders are Under-shepherds. The church's problem, then, is to have only good shepherds rather than hirelings who seek financial gain and personal notoriety to the neglect of proper attention to the sheep.

Preaching the Parable

1. Pastor Jesus. Since "pastor" is a Latin word for "shepherd," it is as appropriate to say "Pastor Jesus" as to say "Jesus is my shepherd." Jesus is a pastor, and he is *my* pastor. This Good Shepherd parable describes God's relationship with his people since it tells us what kind of a pastor we have in Jesus.

A pastor who cares enough to die for us — vv. 11, 15, 17
A pastor who knows us — v. 14
A pastor who wants to care for all the people — v. 16.
A pastor who rose from the dead to be our pastor today —
    vv. 17, 18

2. The One and Only Shepherd. In this parable, Jesus twice says, "I am the good shepherd." We Christians can therefore say about Jesus what David said about Goliath's sword, "There is none like that." (1 Samuel 21:9) Jesus is not merely one of many shepherds, but he alone is the shepherd of all humankind, because he is God's "beloved Son" announced at his baptism and confirmed at the Transfiguration. His death and resurrection made possible the redemption of our sinful world, and in today's First Lesson, we hear

Peter proclaim to the religious leaders of Israel that "there is salvation in no one else."

In an age of pluralism, this claim of Jesus' unique role as savior for all may be offensive to some. In misguided tolerance, we often hold that all religions are roads to God, while some people claim it is an insult to Jews to witness to them about Christ. One of the reasons the number of overseas missionaries has fallen off so drastically in recent years may be because we no longer believe that Jesus is the only savior. Our interest now seems to be to send abroad food, clothing, and education to lift the standard of living for non-Christian peoples.

3. Three Kinds of Shepherds. The parable tells of both good and bad shepherds, but we should also consider the absence of any shepherd as a relevant case. This leads us to an important question: Which of these three is your shepherd?

> No shepherd — "Like sheep without a shepherd" (Matthew 9:36)
> Bad shepherd — hireling (John 10:12-13)
> Good Shepherd — "I am the good shepherd"

4. Poor Sheep! Human sheep need a great deal of compassion since they are faced with two types of terrible enemies which threaten their very lives.

> External enemy: wolves — predators and poachers
> Internal enemy: hirelings — false shepherds

5. The Willingness to Die. Though Jesus loved life and wanted to live, he says in the parable that he willingly laid down his life on his "own accord." (v. 18) Although other faithful shepherds have certainly lost their lives from the attacks of wild animals or thieves in protection of their sheep, Jesus willingly dies for his sheep. Why?

> Because of his love for his sheep — vv. 13, 15
> Because of his obedience to his Father's will — v. 18

6. A Shepherd for All. There is nothing sectarian or provincial about Jesus, the good shepherd. He is a universal shepherd for sheep of all times and nations. He has sheep other than the Jews (v. 16) and his dream is to have one worldwide flock with one shepherd. In hopes that this dream will become a reality, God's people engage in evangelism and missions in the worldwide mission of the church:

one flock consisting of all peoples under one shepherd, Jesus.

Contact

What does the parable of the Good Shepherd say to our generation — to a secular, industrialized, and technological society? Does the metaphor of a shepherd have any relevance? Does this parable still speak to our moral and spiritual needs?

The Good Shepherd parable speaks to our need for a good leader who is also a good shepherd. Years ago, the world suffered from the leadership of men like Hitler, Mussolini, and Stalin, and today we have a similar problem with dicators like Khomeini and Kadhafi.

A good shepherd also gives us a sense of security which is often lacking in today's culture. How can we find financial security, for example, when banks fail, jobs are lost, and high medical costs take our savings? Even the family seems insecure. Many couples cannot be sure of marital fidelity — recent research indicates that over 50% of married women and over 70% of married men are unfaithful to their spouses — so it's little wonder that nearly half of all marriages end in divorce.

Ours is a hurting world. In America alone 60 million people are physically or mentally disabled, over 13 million are deaf, 10 million are blind, and 2.8 million are institutionalized. Millions of others join these in needing someone to care for them, to love them, help them, and listen to their woes. They all need a good shepherd to bind up their wounds, to comfort them in their worries and to help them in their afflictions and needs.

Illustrative Materials

1. A Shepherd of the World. The Good Shepherd is one who gather the peoples of the world into one flock with one shepherd. (v. 16) Years ago, a Bishop of London was vacationing in Scotland. While walking in a rural area, he saw a Scottish shepherd, and he stopped and talked with him for a while. The Bishop said, "You know, I am a shepherd also." The old shepherd looked at this city stranger dressed in such churchly finery and said, "Oh, is that so? How many sheep do you have?" The Bishop replied, "I think about a million." In amazement, the shepherd asked, "and what in the world do you do at lambin' time?"

2. Hireling or Shepherd? A cartoon shows "Brother Juniper" standing with a shepherd's staff, dressed in shepherd's attire, and saying to a flock looking up at him, "Don't look at me. I'm lost, too!"

3. Anybody Care? The commediene Lilly Tomlin shocks her audience when she suddenly collapses on stage in the middle of her routine. She literally just falls over. After a few moments, while still flat on her back, she says to her audience, "I notice none of you got up to see if anything was wrong." Then with a cynical twist of a well-known phrase, she comments, "Remember, we're all in this — alone!" Certainly a good shepherd could restore the truth of the more familiar reading: Remember, we're all in this *together!*

4. Dying for Others to Live. A forest fire burned over some acreage near a farm and some buildings were destroyed. When the embers cooled, the farmer walked around surveying the damage. Noticing a burned lump on the ground, he stoked it with his stick. It was a hen burned to death. When he turned it over, he was surprised when three little chicks ran out terrified and chirping. The hen had died in the flames but somehow had saved her chicks. She died that they might live.

5. Being Died For. One afternoon, in the Spring of 1986, a mentally disturbed member of the world's largest Methodist church came to the church office to shoot the senior pastor, Dr. William Hinson. Since he was not in the church office at the time, the young man went to the office of an associate pastor, Eric Anderson, and killed him. He was shot as a substitute for the senior pastor. Dr. Hinson probably asked himself, "Am I worthy of being died for?" The Good Shepherd died for us — are we worth it?

Easter 5

3. The True Vine

John 15:1-8

[1]*"I am the true vine, and my Father is the vinedresser.* [2]*Every branch of mine that bears no fruit, he takes away, and every branch that does bear fruit, he prunes that it may bear more fruit.* [3]*You are already made clean by the word which I have spoken to you.* [4]*Abide in me, and I in you. As the branch cannot bear fruit by itself, unless it abides in the vine, neither can you unless you abide in me.* [5]*I am the vine, you are the branches. He who abides in me, and I in him, he it is that bears much fruit, for apart from me you can do nothing.* [6]*If a man does not abide in me, he is cast forth as a branch and withers; and the branches are gathered, thrown into the fire and burned.* [7]*If you abide in me, and my words abide in you, ask whatever you will, and it shall be done for you.* [8]*By this my Father is glorified, that you bear much fruit, and so prove to be my disciples."*

A few years ago, PBS presented a TV series, "The Great Search," which examined world religions. One episode showed pictures taken of an Eastern Orthodox Church in Romania, and one of the pictures depicted Christ seated on an altar. From him came a vine with many clusters of grapes which he was shown crushing for the wine of the Holy Eucharist. In today's parable, Jesus similarly claims to be the true vine who gives strength to the branches for bearing fruit to the glory of God.

But is this passage of Scripture truly a parable? Many authorities do not consider "Jesus the True Vine" to be a parable. The author of the Fourth Gospel in the King James and Good News versions, however, refer to "Jesus the Good Shepherd" (John 10:6) as a "parable," and since the accounts of Jesus as the Good Shepherd and Vine are similar, then surely it too can be properly interpreted as a parable. The Good Shepherd parable is pastoral while the other uses agrarian motifs to identify Jesus and his followers, and the figure of the vine certainly is treated as an analogy or metaphor. Allegory is also used — e.g., Jesus calls himself the vine, and compares God the Father to the gardener or the vinedresser and God's people to the branches of the vine. The parable defines the identities of the Father, Son, and believers, and tells us that we must remain attached to the vine, to be fruitful. The life of the branches is derived from the Vine, for from the Vine comes the strength to bear fruit. To be detached from the Vine, furthermore, results not only in non-productivity but also in destruction of the branches by fire. Surely these important elements — metaphor, allegory, an important vital theme — are sufficient to establish John 15 as a parable for our purposes.

Context

Context of the Season

The parable of the Vine is the Gospel for the Fifth Sunday of Easter, so we are still celebrating the triumphant resurrection. What does John 15:1-8 have to do with the empty tomb and the resurrected Christ? Why was this passage chosen for this Sunday of the Easter season?

One possible reason may be that Jesus is an eternal Vine. He is not merely a vine of the past and is certainly not a dead vine. And because of Easter, he is the living Vine for all ages. Because he lives today our branches get their life and strength from him. If the vine were dead, then there would be no hope of eternal life for the branches, and we would still be in our sins. The Cross would only be a sign of martyrdom rather than of salvation. But because the Vine lives, the branches in him produce fruit to the glory of God. On this Fifth Sunday of Easter, therefore, we are proclaiming that the Risen Lord is an eternal Vine to whom we are attached for life and service.

Another reason for the timing of this reading may be found in the words of Jesus, "I am the true vine." Jesus says "am," not "was" nor "will be." The Resurrection enables him to be the reality of our lives today; he is the great "I am," the living one, the alpha and the omega of our existence. "Jesus Christ the same yesterday, today, and forever" is the theme of the Easter season, and Easter 5 is celebrating this eternal truth.

Context of the Day

The Lessons and Propers for Easter 5 focus on Christ the true vine. On this Sunday we deal with the living Christ, and our living in him.

The Prayer of the Day supports the motif of the Vine and branches: "O God, form the minds of your faithful people into a single will. Make us love what you command and desire what you promise . . . " When we abide in Christ, we have his will to love what he commands us to love, and to desire what he promises. So here we pray that our hearts may be in Christ where true joy can be found.

The Hymn of the Day, "Amid the World's Bleak Wilderness," is a contemporary hymn written after 1929, and may not be in older hymnals. It is a retelling of the Vine and branches and ends:
> "Vine, keep what I was meant to be:
> Your branch, with your rich life in me."

Context of the Lectionary

The three Lessons of the Lectionary deal with the living Christ and our living in him.

The First Lesson. (Acts 8:26-40) Philip brings an Ethiopian into the Christian faith. The Lesson tells us how a person becomes one in Christ through the Word and Sacrament of Baptism. Philip explains and interprets the Isaian prophecy of the Lamb. The eunuch accepts the truth and Philip baptizes him into Christ.

The Second Lesson. (1 John 4:7-12) "Abide in me, and I in you," Jesus said. What does it mean to abide in him? Lesson 2 answers that to abide in Christ is to abide in love, for God is love. If we love God and our fellow human beings, then God (Christ) abides in us. This is how we can know that we abide in Christ: we love God and each other.

Gospel (John 15:1-8) Jesus declares that he is the true vine, and that his Father is the gardener or vinedresser who prunes the branches which bear fruit and who cuts off the barren branches.

15:3 — Christ cleanses the branches by his word.

15:4-5 — We read that bearing fruit depends on the branches being in the vine.

15:6 — We see that failure to bear fruit results in destruction.

15:7-8 — We hear the benefits of remaining in Christ the Vine: answered prayer, glorification of the Father, and proof of discipleship.

The Lectionary for Easter 5 needs to be seen in light of both the previous and the upcoming Sundays. Last Sunday, we dealt with the Good Shepherd while next Sunday (Easter 6) the Gospel continues where Easter 5's Gospel ends so that it continues the theme of abiding in Christ. To abide in Christ means to keep his commandment to love each other, and answers the question, "What is the fruit that the branches in the Vine produce?" If a preacher plans to preach on the Gospel for Easter 6, the sermon will simply be a continuation of Easter 5's Gospel lesson. However, because Easter 6 precedes Ascension Day (Holy Thursday), if an Ascension service is not held on Thursday, the festival may then be observed on Easter 6 or 7. (Although Easter 6 is perhaps the better choice so that the Ascension will not come as an anticlimax.)

Context of the Scriptures

The vine was a common symbol in Israel's history, for the vine often represented Israel itself. Near the Holy Place in the Temple, for example, there was a great golden vine. Just as the shepherd and sheep were common in Israel, so in this agricultural age the vine was as familiar a sight as today's apple or peach trees are to us.

After the Flood, Noah planted a vineyard, made wine, and got drunk. (Genesis 9:20) In 1 Kings 21 we find the story of Naboth's vineyard found next to the King Ahab's palace. To acquire this vineyard, Queen Jezebel had Naboth murdered and then had her husband Ahab take possession of the vineyard. Psalm 80 speaks of Israel as the vine which Yahweh brought out of Egypt and caused to flourish even though the vine was ravaged, burned, and cut down.

Israel was also seen as a vine by several of the prophets. Isaiah, for example, speaks of Israel as Yahweh's vineyard which produced wild grapes and, as a result, was laid waste. (Isaiah 5:1-7) Jeremiah has Yahweh say, "Yet I planted you a choice vine, wholly of pure seed. How then have you turned degenerate and become a wild vine?" (Jeremiah 2:21) Ezekiel points out that the wood of the vine is good only for firewood and that Israel will likewise be consumed. (Ezekiel 15; 19:10-14) Hosea calls Israel a luxuriant vine, but notes that the more fruit that was produced also resulted in more altars to false gods.

Jesus also uses the vine in his teachings. In addition to John 15, Jesus tells a parable about workers in a vineyard. (Matthew 20:1) At the Last Supper, Jesus says to the Disciples, "I tell you I shall not drink again of the fruit of the vine until that day when I drink it anew with you in my Father's kingdom." (Matthew 26:29) Jesus passed the cup, filled with the fruit of the vine, saying, "This cup is the new convenant in my blood." In the light of this review, it is most appropriate for Jesus to liken himself and his people to a vine and its branches.

Content

Precis

I am the true vine and my Father is the gardener who removes every branch that does not bear fruit and prunes those that do in order that they may be even more productive. My words have cleansed you that you may be in me. Remain in me as I remain in you and you will produce fruit. A branch cannot bear fruit unless it is attached to the vine. I am the vine and you are the branches. Apart from me you can bear no fruit and you will wither and die, for fruitless branches are thrown into the fire. But if you remain in me, your prayers will be answered regardless of what you ask. By bearing fruit, you glorify God the Father and prove you are my disciples.

Thesis — Doing for Jesus depends upon being and remaining in Jesus.

Theme — Living in Jesus is living for Jesus.

Key Words in the Parable

1. True (v. 1) As we found the good shepherd contrasted with the bad shepherds who do not care for the sheep, so Jesus here claims to be the "true" vine in contrast to false vines. The Greek word, "alethinos," means true, real, and genuine. In the Old Testament, the vine was often associated with degeneration and the failure of Israel, so that God's vine (Israel) became a wild vine and produced wild grapes. And just as the wood of the vine was good only for firewood, so God would throw Israel into the fire of captivity. Hosea reports that when the vine of Israel became luxuriant, idolatry increased. But as the true vine, Christ will give life to the branches. Previously, therefore, Israel was seen as a wild vine and Yahweh had to destroy it because of the unfaithfulness expressed in the wild grapes of wickedness. Now, however, God's Son is the healthy vine which will not fail to be faithful to God and supportive of the branches.

2. Clean (v.3) This verse may be the most difficult one to understand. The Greek word "katharos" (catharsis) is the same word which is also used in the account of Jesus' washing the Disciples' feet at the Last Supper. "Clean" may therefore be best understood in light of the foregoing "prune." When Jesus spoke these words in John 15, Judas Iscariot then left the Upper Room to betray him. To be in and to remain in Christ is to be clean from sin since sin and righteousness cannot exist together, just as oil and water cannot mix. Before being united with Christ, therefore, we are to be cleansed by his word of forgiveness. Today this cleansing is received by the Word in baptism since the water of baptsim symbolizes the spiritual cleansing, and we are made one with Christ by the Word connected with baptism. In Ephesians 5:26 Paul explains, "that he might sanctify her (the church), having cleansed her by the washing of water with the word" (baptism). Through the sacrament of baptism, we are cleansed of our sin and united with Christ.

3. Vinedresser (v. 1) God the Father is the divine gardener whose work it is to dress the vine by coming with a blade to cut and prune the branches. In this parable, then, the branches represent God's people who are part of the Vine. Christians are subject to two different kinds of discipline. On the one hand, certain branches are "pruned" so that they will be even more productive; on the other hand, non-productive branches are cut off from Christ and destroyed in God's judgment upon sterility. This disciplining function of God

is often overlooked or denied. When suffering, hardship, or tragedy occurs, we often confidently say, "This is not God's will." It
may not be, but who is to say this misfortune or suffering is not
God's will?" Perhaps it is God's way of having us become more
fruitful, or it could be God's judgment on our failure to be and do
what he expects of us. It should be noted that the harsher penalty
of destruction is not visited upon those who bear wild grapes, but
upon those who bear no grapes at all.

4. Abide (v. 4) Christ asks us to "abide" in him as he abides
in us. It is one thing to *be* in Christ but another to *remain* in Christ.
Christ's abiding in and with us is not in question, for Christ is forever
faithful and will be with us always. On the other hand we do have
the problem of maintaining our baptismal relationship with Christ.
The loss of faith, apathy, a laxity of duty in performing church
responsibilities — these threaten our deeper need to abide and remain in Christ. To maintain the necessary oneness, we must engage
in prayer, worship, solitude, silence, meditation, and reflection on
God's Word.

5. "Whatever" (v. 7) This word is probably the most compre-
hensive in the passage. To remain in Christ brings this wonderful
promise that "whatever" we ask in prayer will be granted. The context of "whatever" is found in the words, "If you abide in me,"
for when we are in Christ, we will naturally ask for only those bless-
ings that harmonize with God's will. Because we are in Christ, we
will know the will of God and we will want to see it done; so we
will not ask from selfish desires. As a result our prayers will be answered. This is one of the special privileges to be granted in being
one with Christ.

Contemplation

Basic Issues of the Parable

1. Being and Doing. The parable places an equal emphasis upon
both "being" and "doing." We are to be in Christ, and we are to
perform his will that we might be fruitful. In recent years we may
have emphasized "doing" — in terms of social action or exercise

of the social Gospel — to the neglect of "being" as the deeper source of our doing good and serving. The church's primary responsibility and challenge is to be in Christ and to bring others into the same being. If the doing is lacking, therefore, we need to look to our being to see if our relationship with Christ is wanting.

2. Omission and Commission. This parable says much about the sins of omission — i.e., of not yielding fruit, of being largely barren and empty. No mention is made of sins of commission in terms of wild or sour grapes or wickedness, but the barren branches are cut off and thrown into the fire. It is the lack of rendering service which is treated most seriously by God, and this might lead us to conclude that our sins of ommision are more important than the sins of commission.

3. Branches and the Vine. The branches (people) are connected with the Vine (Christ). There are two kinds of branches in the parable. One category includes the branches that are pruned in order to bear more fruit, while the other type consists of branches that are barren and are cut off and burned. Both types, however, are branches that are attached to Christ the Vine, so here we are dealing with church people, not with non-Christians. The parable also says that salvation is not to be found in any other religion, for Christ is *the* true vine, and there is no other vine. It is necessary to be attached to the vine to live since to be detached because of fruitlessness leads to destruction.

4. Abide in Christ. It is one thing to be in or attached to Christ the Vine, and it is quite another to remain in Christ. For all people to *become* one in Christ demands evangelism and missions, but it is an equally important task to enable those already in Christ to "abide" and remain in Christ. This task calls for loyalty and faithfulness under all conditions and for all time. The recent declines in mainline Protestant membership should call our attention to the fact that many people have failed to remain in Christ, and suggests that perhaps the greatest mission today is to be found in the church itself rather than outside her.

5. Fate of the Fruitless. Jesus described the Father as the vinedresser or gardener who comes to the vineyard with an axe or blade. Discipline of the fruitful branches is exerted by pruning, and judgment comes to the fruitless who are to be cut off from Christ and destroyed by fire. We must not ignore this part of the parable simply out of fear that it may be discomforting to the "good" people in the pews. The parable is simply saying, "Be fruitful — or else!"

6. Discipline of Disciples. In the parable, no branch in the Vine goes untouched since every branch is either cut back or cut off. Of the two alternatives, the former is certainly preferred. Pruning is not an easy or comfortable experience, and may it mean pain, loss, suffering, defeat, or tragedy, but it also suggests the biblical saying, "Whom the Lord loves, he chastens even as a father chastens his son," because the purpose of the discipline is to enable the branch to bear more fruit. Out of adversity, struggle, and sorrow we may find a deeper character and often a closer walk with God.

Preaching the Parable

1. All That a Christian Ought to Be. What does it take to be a true Christian? There are so many different kinds of Christians that we may have difficulty in knowing whether we are genuine Christians. The parable gives us the components of a true Christian who:
Accepts the discipline of pruning — vv. 2, 6
Remains in Christ the Vine — v. 4
Is fruitful in the quality of life and service — vv. 5, 8

2. Life in the Living Christ. In this Easter season, the Risen Christ is in our consciousness. He is the living Vine to which we are joined and in which we live. What is this life in Christ?
A life of prayer — v. 7
A life of service — v. 8
A life of glorifying God — v. 8

3. Essentials of the Christian Life. Today's parable gives us the basics for a Christian life:
Being in Christ — v. 5
Remaining in Christ — v. 4
Doing for Christ — v. 5
Being in Christ begins at baptism. As an act of God's grace, a person is intitiated, incorporated, and inducted into the Kingdom.

Paul speaks of the Gentiles being "grafted" into the olive tree, while the branch of the Jews was broken off due to their lack of belief. (Romans 11:17-24)

Remaining in Christ calls for persistence and loyalty until death.

Doing for Christ means finding the strength to grow and bear fruit.

4. The Problem of Fruitfulness.

    A. *The impossibility of being fruitful when detached from the vine* — vv. 4, 6. Apart from Christ we are nothing, and we can do nothing good in God's sight. When a branch is cut off from the vine, it withers and dies, and then is thrown into the fire.

    B. *The possibilty of being attached to the vine and yet not fruitful* — v. 2. Nominal Christians and inactive members of the church are still attached to the vine, but they are unfruitful. Evidence of this is to be found in their low quality of life, their neglect of the church, and their failure to perform service. In the parable, of course, Jesus taught that these barren branches will be destroyed.

5. Keeping in Touch with Christ.
People usually seem to recognize the need to keep in touch with each other. If friends fail to do this, for example, they eventually become strangers to each other, while workers often keep in touch with the central office by means of shortwave radios. Jesus tells us to "abide," to remain in touch with him. (v. 4)

How does one keep in touch with Christ from day to day?

    Public worship
    Bible reading
    Personal devotions: solitude, prayer, meditation

6. Blessings of Abiding in Christ.
Does any good come from being and remaining in Christ? Are there any rewards? What would it profit a person to be and remain in Christ? Let the parable answer:

    It makes us fruitful — vv. 4-5

    It saves us from destruction — v. 6

    It answers our prayers — v. 7

    It glorifies God — v. 8

Contact

Problems

Preachers again face the problem of making an agricultural concept meaningful to people in a largely urban, commercial, and industrial society. This same problem was confronted in the parable
of the Good Shepherd. How many church people are familiar with
a vineyard? Must we go to the vineyards of California, New York,
France, or Italy to make the parable meaningful? The challenge we
face is to proclaim the principles and truth which the metaphor
defines.

The similarity of last Sunday's parable of the Good Shepherd
to today's parable of the True Vine may also cause concern to the
preacher. Both parables, for example, deal with the identity of Jesus
and there is also a similarity in the description offered of Jesus as
"good" and "true." Is there enough difference between the two
parables, therefore, to avoid mere duplication? The special quality
of the Vine parable may be that it defines a mystical relationship
in which a person becomes one with the Savior, remains in him, and
derives strength from him to serve.

Need

Before writing the sermon, we need to be certain whether the truth
of the parable is needed by today's congregation. Are today's church
people truly living in the eternal Christ? In 1985 a survey was made
of 2500 Protestants regarding their devotional practices, and revealed that 49% had a prayer of thanks before meals, 57% prayed
daily, 24% read the Bible several times a week, and only 8% had
family devotions. From these statistics, we can easily see that a majority of church members are most obviously not "abiding" in Christ.
When half do not pray daily, three-quarters do not read the Bible,
92% do not have family devotions, 70% do not regularly worship,
and 40% do not receive the Holy Communion at least annually, then
there is a clear reason for the church's decline in membership, the
apathy of those who remain and the lack of service to humanity by
all concerned. Perhaps, then, the parable of the Vine is more relevant today than it has ever been.

To abide in Christ the Vine requires the very same personal and family devotions which we have just seen to be neglected by a majority of Christians. The neglect may be due to busy schedules and involvement in all kinds of secular activities since it is difficult for a person in today's crowded world to find the time and place for solitude, silence, and prayer alone with God. For many people, therefore, perhaps devotions and contemplation need not be as structured or restrictive as in the past. Solitude, silence, meditation, reflection, and prayer might well be held during the night when it is difficult to go to sleep or in the morning while waiting for a spouse to wake up. We can think seriously about God and life while having a second cup of coffee in the mornings, or while stuck in bumper-to-bumper traffic or when doing repetitive manual activity such as sewing, cooking, washing the car, watering the lawn, or vacuuming the carpets. And while waiting to enter a hospital room, standing in line to check out the week's groceries, or taking your turn to get into the doctor's inner office, you might occupy your mind with more vital matters than listening to the Muzak.

Illustrative Materials

1. A Fruitful Life. Recently I was in a living room where there was a handmade banner which displayed a plant and the verse, "By this my Father is glorified, that you bear much fruit." (John 15:8) It was given by the staff of the Lutheran Church in America to my close friend of more than 50 years, Dr. Robert W. Stackel, at the time of his retirement. It was an appropriate gift to a man who had produced much fruit for the Kingdom as director of the Lutheran Evangelism Mission, executive director of Lutheran World Missions, and leader of the Lutheran Hunger Appeal which raised millions of dollars to feed the starving. And what was the secret of his fruitfulness? Simply that not a day passes without reading the Bible and spending time in prayer.

2. Care of the Inside. There is a TV commercial for Kellogg's cereals in which a young man is shown doing his daily calisthenics to strengthen his body and build muscle. His wife comes to him with a box of cereal and urges him to eat the cereal to care for his insides as well. Much attention and effort are given today to bodybuilding by "pumping iron," aerobics, and jazzercise, but little attention is given to inner spiritual development of the soul. We must also "take care of the inside."

3. How Close to God? Two women spent much of an afternoon trying to impress each other with how religious each was. When the visit was over, one said to her husband — who had overheard the discussion and who was quietly smoking his pipe — "You know, Mrs. Sills is a good Christian, but I just believe I live closer to the Lord." After thinking a moment, he replied, "Ain't either of you crowding him any!"

4. Keep in Touch. "Abide in me" means to keep in touch with Christ. Recently a Viet-Nam Memorial was dedicated in Washington. It is a curved wall with more than 58,000 names of fallen veterans carved into the black marble, and thousands of spouses, sweethearts, parents, children, and war buddies came to find the name of a loved one and touch the name. As their fingers went over the name they wept, sobbed, or prayed. It was their way to once again be in touch with a loved one.

5. Don't Leave Me. Jesus urged his Disciples to abide in him, to remain in him, and to be loyal to him. At the age of 86, a retired university professor was dying in a hospital. By this age she had outlived most of her friends and associates, and her former students were unaware of her condition and loneliness. Her minister visited, but he was too busy to spend more than a few minutes with her when he came. One day, as the minister began to leave, she reached for the hand of her nurse and implored, "Don't leave me." Jesus also reaches out for us and asks us to join him.

6. Living but Dead. Three peasants were once walking on a country road, when to their amazement, they came upon a man lying on the road. They looked him over and he appeared to be healthy and to have a good robust color. He seemed to be well fed, and his clothes were of fine quality. He looked intelligent. So they decided there was nothing wrong with him, and to put him on his feet and let him go his way. They stood him up — but he fell over. They did this three times and each time he fell over. Finally they concluded, "There is nothing wrong with this man, but he won't stand up." And this is the sorry state of the barren branches in the parable as well — to be alive but never know the beauty of fruitfulness to be found in service to Christ.

Proper 5 • Pentecost 3 • Ordinary Time 10

Common   Lutheran   Roman Catholic

4. A Strong Man

Mark 3:20-25

20The crowd came together again, so that they could not even eat. 21And when his family heard it, they went out to seize him, for people were saying, "He is beside himself." 22And the scribes who came down from Jerusalem said, "He is possessed by Beelzebub, and by the prince of demons he casts out the demons." 23And he called them to him, and said to them in parables, "How can Satan cast out Satan? 24If a kingdom is divided against itself, that kingdom cannot stand. 25And if a house is divided against itself, that house will not be able to stand. 26And if Satan has risen up against himself and is divided, he cannot stand, but is coming to an end. 27But no one can enter a strong man's house and plunder his goods, unless he first binds the strong man; then indeed he may plunder his house.

28Truly, I say to you, all sins will be forgiven the sons of men, and whatever blasphemies they utter, 29but whoever blasphemes against the Holy Spirit never has forgiveness, but is guilty of an eternal sin" — 30for they had said, "He has an unclean spirit."

31And his mother and his brothers came; and standing outside they sent to him and called him. 32And a crowd was sitting about him, and they said to him, "Your mother and your brothers are outside, asking for you." 33And he replied, "Who are my mother and my brothers?" 34And looking around on those who sat about him, he said, "Here are my mother and my brothers! 35Whoever does the will of God is my brother, and sister, and mother."

"Why is this man so popular?" "This question appeared on the cover of *Time* magazine beside a smiling picture of President Ronald Reagan. Inside the magazine many facts were presented to help prove that he is indeed very popular in America. According to a Gallup poll taken after six years of his presidency, sixty-eight percent of the American people approved of his leadership, and he has had a higher rating over a longer period of time than any other second-term president since such polling began.

The feature article goes on to tell us that he is so popular especially because of the relative success of his presidency, because he is proving to be one of the strongest leaders of the twentieth century, because he restored the prestige and authority of the Office of the Presidency, because of his deep personal authenticity, and because during his term America has had an economic recovery lasting over forty-three months — the longest in our history.

Why is this man Jesus so popular? Jesus did not have a national periodical like *Time* to analyze his popularity, but it nevertheless was a matter of great concern to many. Multitudes came to hear, teach, and preach, and many came to be healed. Evil spirits were driven out by the authority of his word and by the power of God. He was extraordinarily popular beyond all doubt — but why? Certainly it was largely due to his miracles and teaching. But how was he able to cast out demons? Such actions obviously required supernatural power, but was it the power of God or of Satan? Scribes speaking for the day's religious leaders claimed Jesus used the power of Satan but in answer to this charge, Jesus defended himself with the parables of the divided kingdom and the strong man. In this chapter, we will deal with both parables and with the circumstances surrounding them as given in today's Gospel Lesson, Mark 3:20-35.

Context

Context of the Church Season and Day

The parables for this third Sunday after Pentecost (Proper 5) take us into the Pentecost season, the last and longest season of the church year. It is the season of the Holy Spirit, and it is also the season of the church since it is the Spirit which creates the church. Over a period of 28 Sundays, we deal with the work, gifts, and fruit of the Spirit, and during this period we should consider the teachings and the mighty acts of God in Christ. It is a time of growth — growth in mind, heart, and spirit. And it is because green is the color of growth that the liturgical color of the Pentecost season is green.

During the Pentecost season, there is no especial significance to the Sundays, and when a minor or major festival falls on one, the festival takes precedence over the ordinary Sunday.

In the Pentecost season, there is no clearly defined theme that binds together the Lessons, Psalm, Prayer and Hymn of the Day. The Psalm usually harmonizes with the First Lesson, and the Prayer and Hymn invariably deal with the Gospel. For thirteen Sundays the First Lesson gives biographical accounts of David. Over a period of twenty-six Sundays the Second Lesson consists of readings from four of the Epistles. Except for eight Sundays, the Gospels are taken from Mark. This wide variety of Scripture selections gives us a broad choice of texts and subjects

Context of the Lectionary

As we have just seen, each Lesson is independent of the other two because they were not chosen on a thematic basis. Nevertheless, the Lessons certainly do not contradict each other, and, indeed, several similarities can perhaps be found.

The First Lesson. (1 Samuel 16:14-23) King Saul was tormented by an evil spirit, so his servants suggested that he get someone to play the lyre for him. David was highly recommended so Saul sent for him. David entered Saul's service, and his playing refreshed Saul so that the evil spirit left him. In today's Gospel, Jesus is accused of being insane and of using the devil to exorcise evil spirits. But Jesus was not a son of Saul but, rather, a son of the David who possessed the spirit of the Lord. It was by the power of God, therefore, that David's son, Jesus, exorcised evil spirits.

The Second Lesson. (2 Corinthians 4:13—5:1) Paul is telling about the hardships of his ministry, but all of his suffering is for the sake of the Corinthian Christians. Both Paul and the Corinthians have the same spirit, the same faith, the same hope of eternal life, and the same grace. There is here a connection with the Gospel in which Jesus speaks of the fall of a divided kingdom and house. If Jesus were in league with the devil, then Satan's house would be divided against itself and would fall. But just as Paul and the Corinthians have oneness, so the Father and Jesus are one.

Gospel. (Mark 3:20-35) Jesus was immensely popular because of his teaching and miracles. The crowd was so demanding of him that there was no time for him even to eat. The people began saying Jesus was crazy. This caused Jesus' family to find him and to take him away from the violent crowds. The scribes held that Jesus drove out demons by the power of Satan, but in response Jesus tells the parable about a kingdom, which if divided falls. He also tells a second parable of a strong man overcome. Jesus goes on to say that to claim that Jesus is a devil is to commit the unpardonable sin. When his family arrives, Jesus is told that his mother and brothers are outside waiting for him, and he reveals that his family consists of all who do the will of God.

> 3:20-22 — the situation: charges against Jesus by people and scribes.
>
> 3:23-26 — parable of the divided kingdom and house.
>
> 3:27 — parable of the strong man.
>
> 3:28-30 — The unpardonable sin of saying that Jesus has an unclean spirit.
>
> 3:31-34 — Arrival of Jesus' family to take him home.

Context of the Scriptures

1. Mark. Today's gospel does not give the background or the setting for the parables. In Mark 3:7-12, however, we learn of the great extent of Jesus' popularity. A great multitude followed Jesus to the Sea of Galilee, and people came from all over Judea, Jerusalem, Idumea, Tyre, and Sidon. The crowd was so great that Jesus had to borrow a boat lest the crowd push him into the lake. Christ healed various diseases and cast out unclean spirits. After selecting his disciples, he journeyed home (Capernaum), but the crowd gathered again at his house. It is at this point that the Gospel for the Day begins.

2. Parallel Passages. (Matthew 12:22-32; Luke 11:14-23) Since these parallel passages are not used elsewhere in the Lectionary in the near future, a preacher may make use of them here to further clarify the parables of the divided kingdom and the strong man.

In Matthew, Jesus heals a blind and dumb man who was demon possessed. This caused the *Pharisees* to charge Jesus with being in league with Beelzebub.

In Luke, Jesus heals a man who was speechless, and some of the *people* claim Jesus did it by the power of Beelzebub.

How does Mark's account differ from Matthew's and Luke's?

A. Only Mark involves Jesus' family in the incident.

    B. Matthew and Luke give the setting of the accusation: the casting out of a demon from a sick person.

    C. The charge that Jesus was an agent of Satan was made by the Pharisees in Matthew, by some of the people in Luke, and by the scribes in Mark.

    D. In Matthew and Luke, Jesus argues that the religious leaders of the day also cast out demons. Would his accusers claim, Jesus asks, that these leaders were agents of Satan? If not, then why is Jesus to be so accused?

Content

The Gospel for this Sunday may be confusing because there are two parables in the pericope. The two are related to each other, however, and the parables are related to the pericope. At first sight we might wonder why the various items are placed together in the same pericope, but preaching on the parable of the strong man we must be certain to deal with the entire pericope, because the various items are connected with each other.

First, there is the immense popularity of Jesus' miracles, and this raises the question of how he performed them. All agree that he has supernatural power, but great disagreement is expressed over whether the power is of God or of Satan.

Second, there are the reactions to his popularity and to his miraculous power of casting out demons. Some people say that he is out of his mind, while the scribes say Christ is an agent of Satan. These accusations cause his family to come to rescue him from the crowd.

Third, Jesus defends himself against the charge of the scribes, and he answers them with the two parables. In the first, Jesus points out of that fate of a divided kingdom or house must be to fall. He reasons from this that if he were in league with Satan and yet doing good by casting out demons, it would indicate that Satan's kingdom would be divided since Jesus would be doing good while Satan does only evil. The parable of the strong man then states that a strong man can still be overcome. Jesus does not say explicitly that he is stronger than Satan, but he clearly implies that he is more powerful. By driving out demons, for example, he proves that he has overcome Beelzebub.

Fourth, Jesus shows how serious is the accusation that he operates as an agent of Satan. He declares that the sin of saying that Jesus has an unclean spirit is unpardonable.

Fifth, by the time Jesus' family has arrived they cannot get into the house to confer with Jesus because of the crowd. Others tell him that his mother and brothers are outside, and in response Christ gives a new understanding of his family — i.e., those who do the will of God are his mother, brothers, and sisters.

Precis

A large crowd came to Jesus for healing. He and his disciples were so busy they had no time for meals. His family heard people saying that he lost his mind. Professional Bible teachers — i.e., Scribes — came from Jerusalem to claim that Jesus cast out demons by the power of Satan. To defend himself against this charge, Jesus gave the scribes two parables. One said that a divided kingdom or house could not stand. If he cast out demons by Satan, Satan would be working against himself, and his kingdom would come to an end. Another parable was about a strong man conquered by a stronger man. It is implied that the stronger man is Jesus who overcomes the strong man, Satan, by evicting demons. To say that Jesus is an agent of Satan is so serious that it is an unpardonable sin. By this time Jesus' family had arrived but could not get into the house where Jesus was teaching and healing. When Jesus was told that his family was outside, he replied that his family consists of all those who do the will of his Father.

Thesis: By the power of God, the strong man, Satan, is overcome by the stronger one, Jesus.

Theme: Jesus is stronger than all evil.

Key Words in the Parable

1. "Beside himself" (v. 21) Many people claimed that Jesus was insane. So serious and pervasive was this charge that Jesus' family came to take him home to Nazareth away from the crowds. Could this mean that his mother, brothers, and sisters were ashamed of him, or were they concerned only for his safety?

It is not unusual for deeply committed Christians to be termed insane or mad. Festus said to Paul, for example, "Paul, you are mad; your great learning is turning you mad." (Acts 26:24) Paul writes that it is quite all right to be mad for God: "If we are beside ourselves, it is for God; if we are in our right mind it is for you." (2 Corinthians 5:13)

From a secular viewpoint, Jesus could possibly be considered to be out of his mind. He certainly seems crazy to get so involved with people's needs and problems that there is no time for him even to eat. Moreover, it is at least a little crazy to get involved with demon-possessed people since good sense would dictate that the problems of normal people are difficult enough to solve. And, ironically, it was Jesus' healing of evil-spirited people which resulted in Jesus' being accused of being an agent of Satan. But, in the final analysis, we can only say that Jesus was "crazy" in that he had the strength to do what he knew what must be done even though he also knew that such extreme dedication would brand him as insane in the eyes of those who didn't understand his mission.

2. "Possessed by Beelzebub" (v. 22) Beelzebub was a Syrian god. In 2 Kings 1:2, for example, we read that when Ahaziah, king of Israel, fell off the roof of his palace, he sent representatives to ask Beelzebub, god of Ekron, whether he would recover. Among Israelites, however, Beelzebub was a name for the devil.

Why would religious leaders of Jesus' day conclude that Jesus was an agent of Satan? Consider the following:

Mark 2:15-17 — Jesus kept company with publicans and sinners.

2:18-22 — Jesus refused to have his disciples fast as John the Baptizer's disciples did.

2:23-28 — Jesus violated Sabbath laws.

3:1-6 — Jesus healed on the Sabbath day.

3:7-12 — Unclean spirits witnessed to Jesus as Son of God.

3. "Divided" (v. 24) Jesus answered the charge of the scribes by pointing out that a divided kingdom or family cannot stand. If it were true, in other words, that Jesus was casting out demons by Beelzebub, it would then mean that Satan's kingdom was divided against itself. Satan works only for evil; Jesus works only for good.

Unity is one of the goals of Jesus' ministry. In Ephesians, Paul emphasizes the oneness we have in Christ, and says that His coming to earth was "to unite all things in him." (Ephesians 1:10) Because of Christ, then, humanity was no longer divided into competing camps of Jews and Gentiles, but were now all members of the church (Ephesians 3:6) By means of the Cross, humanity was united with God, for in Christ God reconciled the world to himself. (2 Corinthians 5:19) Before Christ, we were divided through our hostility toward each other until Christ then became our peace and united us to the Father and to each other in the family of God. Consequently, we have "one Lord, one faith, one baptism." (Ephesians 4:4)

4. "Strong" (v. 27) The second parable in this pericope deals with a strong man overcome by a stronger man. As is customary in many of his parables, Jesus leaves the interpretation of certain aspects up to his audience. Since the demons are exorcised by Jesus, for example, it would imply to us that Jesus is stronger than Satan, king of evil spirits, and this also proves that Jesus is not an agent of Satan, but his conqueror.

God's people are assured in this parable, and throughout Scripture, that God will always be the victor in the end. Yahweh promises, "I will fight against whoever fights you, and I will rescue your children." (Isaiah 49:25) Jesus tells his disciples, "Be brave! I have defeated the world." (John 16:33) At Caesarea Philippi, Jesus promises, "I will build my church and not even death will ever be able to overcome it." In Ephesians, Paul visualizes the ultimate triumph of Christ: "God put all things under Christ's feet and gave him to the church as supreme Lord over all things." (Ephesians 1:22) And in the end, Satan will be destroyed: "The devil who had deceived them was thrown into the lake of fire and brimstone." (Revelation 20:10)

5. "Never" (v. 29) We are often advised to "never say never" — but Jesus did. Anyone who blasphemes the Holy Spirit will "never" be forgiven because it is the unpardonable sin. This causes deep concern for many people because they fear that they may have or will, commit it. Why would Jesus place such powerful emphasis upon this sin? To say that Jesus has an evil spirit rather than the Holy Spirit is to turn him to Satan; to claim, as the scribes did, that he performed miracles by the power of Beelzebub is to do Jesus the worst possible injustice. This is unpardonable because if anyone is of the opinion that Jesus is of Satan then this also claims that Jesus as God's Son did not die for the sins of the world. But since forgiveness is only made possible by the Cross, it would not then be possible to be forgiven. Moreover, because the Holy Spirit is God who convicts us of sin and points us to Christ as Savior, to reject the Holy Spirit means to refuse to be brought to God for forgiveness.

Contemplation

When we reflect upon the context and content of today's Gospel lesson, preachers are faced with the question of what aspect of the pericope should be preached. The choice will probably depend upon the need of the specific congregation, or upon a pressing problem in the community at large. It will would be difficult, however, to preach on just one specific aspect of the pericope because each part is related to the overall theme: does Jesus cast out demons by the power of God or of Satan?

Homily Hints

1. How Do You Account for Jesus' Popularity? Jesus' healing and teaching drew multitudes to him. In ministering to the crowd, he was too busy even to get a bite to eat. He miraculously cast out demons. How do you explain his success? What motivates him? Is his power derived from God or from Satan? In today's Gospel we see several reactions to his ministry:
  A. The crowd said "He is beside himself" — v. 21
  B. Religious leaders said "He has an unclean spirit" — vv. 22, 30
  C. Jesus' family: ashamed of Jesus, they came to take him to seclusion — vv. 21, 31

It needs to be noted that in this account no one has a word of support, defense, or commendation for Jesus. Why were the newly-appointed Disciples silent in the face of the accusations leveled against Jesus? Jesus was forced to defend himself by arguing that he worked by the power of God.

2. Seeing it Whole. The pericope (Mark 3:20-35) tells the whole story surrounding the parables. The parables need to be seen in the light of this context which grants the parables a relevant message. The pericope includes:

    A. The situation — Jesus' popularity resulting from exorcising demons — v. 20.

    B. The charges against him — by the crowd and by scribes — vv. 21-22.

    C. Jesus' defense — two parables — vv. 23-27.

    D. Consequence of the false charge — the unpardonable sin — vv. 28-30.

    E. Status of those who side with Jesus — the family of God — vv. 31-32.

3. One stronger than the Strongest. Jesus tells the parable of a strong man being overcome. By casting out demons, he shows that he is stronger than Satan.

This shows us that Strength is *not* necessarily to be found in:

    A. *Physical strength.* Consider the boy David and the giant Goliath, for example. (1 Samuel 17) Here David said, "This day the Lord will deliver you into my hand."

    B. *Equipment.* David could not even wear Saul's armor, and compare Goliath's mammoth sword with David's tiny sling and five stones.

    C. *Numbers.* Gideon, for example, showed that a dedicated minority of 300 can defeat an army. (Judges 7).

        On the other hand, strength *is* to be found in:

    a. God the Father — "He who is in you is greater than he who is in the world." (1 John 4:4)

    b. God the Son — "I can do all things in him who strengthens me." (Philippians 4:13)

    c. God the Spirit — "God did not give us a spirit of timidity but a spirit of power and love and self-control." (2 Timothy 1:7)

4. The Battle of Life. Life is a battle between good and evil, between Christ and Beelzebub, and it is a neverending fight. The struggle goes on both inside each individual and within society as a whole. The parable of the strong man therefore reflects a familiar situation.

    A. The contest — good or evil, Christ or Satan, truth or falsehood?

        The conflict in Paul's experience — Romans 7:13-25.

B. The conquest — the one who overcomes is Christ, and
we are one in Christ.
Love is stronger than hatred.
Life is stronger than death.
Hope is stronger than despair.
Truth is stronger than falsehood.

5. The Great Divide. In defending himself against the charge that
his casting out of demons indicated that he was in league with Satan, Jesus gave the parable of the divided kingdom and house. He
pointed out that since a divided kingdom must fall, if he were an
agent of Satan exorcising evil spirits, then he would also be working
against Satan. Lincoln made this parable famous when he quoted
it in saying that America could not exist half "slave" and half "free"
and today the same is true with South Africa.

The truth of this parable is expressed in many areas of everyday
life. A divided married couple will eventually be divorced or separated; a divided mind leads to the confusion James wrote about in
noting "A double-minded man, unstable in all his ways . . . " (James
1:8) and even a church can be crippled by internal strife as can be
seen in the split between Fundamentalists and Moderates, or between
Charismatics and Traditionalists. It was because this sort of internal discord was a problem in Paul's churches, that he appealed
"Complete my joy by being of the *same* mind, having the *same* love,
being in full accord and of one mind." (Philippians 2:2)

What is the solution to such separation, schism, or division? It
is, quite simply, being on one side or the other: God's or Satan's.
To serve both is impossible, says Jesus: "You cannot serve God and
mammon." (Matthew 6:24) We must be either for or against Christ
and there is no middle ground. It is only when we are one in Christ
that we will be one with each other; the closer we come to Christ,
the closer we will be to each other.

6. The New Family. Jesus' family has an important role in today's parable. When his mother, brothers, and sisters heard that people were claiming Jesus to be crazy, they came to take him home
to Nazareth. They were seemingly embarrassed by the report and
possibly were even ashamed of him — they wanted to get him out
of the public eye if he were a mad man. When they came to get him,
however, they could not get in the house because it was so crowded.

When word reached Jesus that his family was outside asking for him, he gave us a new concept of family: the family of God.

According to Jesus, God's family:

A. Does *not* consist of —
   a. Only those related by blood.
   b. All those created as humans. All people are human beings but not all are children of God.
   c. Only those of like race or religion.
B. God's family does consist of:
   Those who do the will of God.

7. The Glory of Madness. In today's Gospel, people say about Jesus: "He is mad. He is crazy. He is out of his mind. He is beside himself." Mentally ill people need our help and care, but there is a type of madness that is a glory.

This special kind of madness may take two forms:

First, it may occur when we are mad at the wrongs in our world. It is time that we got "mad" at injustice, poverty, discrimination, pornography, and crime. Paul commanded, "Be angry and sin not." We need to get mad enough to stop the evils of our day.

Second, we may be deemed mad because of the intensity of our devotion and sacrifice for Christ. Paul called himself a "fool" for Christ, for example, and all to Jesus may seem to be crazy to the world at large.

Contact

Points of Contact

Today's lection has four points of relevance to contemporary society and church people.

1. Division. Both the world and our church, experience the problem of disunity. Half of American families are divided by divorce; war signals the lack of unity among nations; strikes indicate that labor and management cannot join in harmony; racial violence reminds us that races may be opposed to each other.

2. Interpretation. How does one explain the marvelous work of Jesus? Is he actually out of his mind — in league with the devil —

or is he an agent of God's power? If we conclude that Jesus exorcises demons by the power of God, then we also obligate ourselves to accept him as Lord.

3. Strength. People want and need strength for their tasks and trials. Our enemy is a strong man, and to overcome him, therefore, we must also be strong. According to the parable, Satan is strong, but the one who invades his stronghold is still able to triumph. Since Jesus drove out the demons leagued with Satan, he is stronger than Satan. People today need the confidence and comfort that God will ultimately win, that people in Christ will have victory over the world. Consider for a moment: How many people who feel themselves to be weak are in your congregation? The parable will speak to them.

4. Family. In today's America, the family is in a crisis — divorce, separation, spouse brutality, child abuse, alcoholism and drugs — all threaten to destroy it. So today's family — as Jesus' family in this pericope — may feel ashamed of Jesus when we are in a crowd.

In this passage, Jesus enlarges his family to include all those who do the will of God. Christ becomes our brother in the family of God, and the church consists of God's family into which we are adopted through baptism. Members of the church are our brothers and sisters because they are in Christ and do the will of God. In a day when 40% of Americans are single, many may feel that they have no family. If they do the will of God, however, they do have a family: the family of God.

Illustrative Materials

1. God or Satan? The scribes claimed that Jesus was possessed by Beelzebub and cast out demons by the power of Satan. John Huss, an early reformer, was burned at the stake in 1415 for his Protestant heresy. Before he was burned to death, his accusers placed a crown of paper with painted devils on his head. In place of a crown of thorns, therefore, Jesus might well have worn the same crown of devils.

2. Who is Stronger? Since a stronger person can overcome a strong one, the goal is for each of us to be the stronger. This is the key to the nuclear arms race. One superpower is ever trying to be stronger than the other to prevent being overcome. Greater nuclear capability is claimed to be a deterrent to a nuclear attack. Dr. Brzezinski, national security adviser in the Carter administration, wrote in a May 1986 periodical:

> We have to face the fact, painful though it may be, that we cannot get rid of nuclear weapons. It is the reality of nuclear weapons that has certainly contributed to an unprecedented degree of restraint in the American and Soviet conduct of the intense and highly conflictual rivalry between the two superpowers. In any other age, these superpowers would have come into direct conflict many times over in the course of the last forty years. It has been the existence of nuclear weapons that has made both sides more prudent, more restrained.

3. Mad. Today's Gospel tells us that many people claimed that Jesus was a "mad" (crazy) man. Mark put it in more respectful words: "He is beside himself." There are times when we *should* be "mad." Mothers, who lost children by a drunken driver, organized themselves into an organization called MADD, "Mothers Against Drunken Drivers." None of them are "crazy" but they're properly "beside themselves" with righteous anger.

Saint John Chrysostom said, "Whoever is without anger, when there is cause for anger, sins."

Addressing a graduation class at the University of Michigan in 1983, Lee Iacocca said, "I want you to get mad about the current state of affairs. I want you to get so mad that you kick your elders in their figurative posteriors and move America off dead center."

Proper 6 • Pentecost 4 • Ordinary Time 11
Common · Lutheran · Roman Catholic

---

5. The Miracle Seed

Mark 4:26-32

---

[26] He said, "The kingdom of God is as if a man should scatter seed upon the ground, [27] and should sleep and rise night and day, and the seed should sprout and grow, he knows not how. [28] The earth produces of itself, first the blade, then the ear, then the full grain in the ear. [29] But when the grain is ripe, at once he puts in the sickle, because the harvest has come."

[30] And he said, "With what can we compare the kingdom of God, or what parable shall we use for it? It is like a grain of mustard seed, which, when sown upon the ground, is the smallest of all the seeds on earth; [32] yet when it is sown it grows up and becomes the greatest of all shrubs, and puts forth large branches, so that the birds of the air can make nests in its shade."

Today's Gospel presents two parables for preaching. This means that we must decide whether or not to prech on both or on just one. The parables presented here are: "The Secretly Growing Seed," (4:26-29) and "The Mustard Seed." (4:30-32)

While each parable carries its own special message, there are similarities between them. Both present a description of the Kingdom of God; both parables involve a growing seed and the size of plant the seed produces. When we think of "seed," we also usually think of the parable of the sower and the soils, but this popular parable will not appear in the Lectionary for almost two years — Pentecost 8-A, Proper 10 — so we need have little fear of repetition in our message.

Another important theme presented is the subject of growth. One of today's parables tells us of a seed's gradual growth while the second amazes us with spectacular growth. Both parables also contrast the tiny seed with the bountiful harvest it is able to produce.

Context

Context of the Day

Since the First and Second Lessons are readings in course, there is no clear relation to the Gospel for the Day. The Psalm (46) is related to the First Lesson and is a lament over Saul and Jonathan's death ("The nations rage, the kingdoms totter." [v. 6]) The Prayer of the Day reminds us that we were called as priests "to bear witness" to God's promises, or, in other words, to scatter the seed of God's Word. The Hymn of the Day, however, is definitely related to the parables of the seed:

"Almighty God, Your Word is cast
Like seed into the ground."

Context of the Lectionary

The First Lesson. (2 Samuel 1:1, 17-27) David laments the death of King Saul and of his dear friend, Jonathan. With their deaths, Saul's kingdom comes to an end and David's kingdom is about to be established. In relation to the day's parables, the death and burial of Saul's kingdom plants the seed for the new and greater kingdom of David.

The Second Lesson. (2 Corinthians 5:1-10, 14-17) Paul assures the Corinthian Church that the physical body will be replaced by a spiritual one. To be in the physical body is also to be separated from Christ, but when physical death gives us a spiritual body, we will be with Christ. God will provide a new body, and in Christ we will form a new creation. In 1 Corinthians 15:35-50 Paul compares the body to the seed. Like seed, he says, the physical body is sown by dying and burial, and from this seed then rises a new body, the spiritual one. Thus, Paul writes, "God gives it a body as he has chosen, and to each kind of *seed* its own body. It is sown a physical body, it is raised a spiritual body." (vv. 38, 44) [author emphasis]

Gospel. (Mark 4:26-34) In two parables, Jesus describes the Kingdom of God. The first parable likens the kingdom to seed that grows secretly until maturity, while the second tells us that the Kingdom of God begins small but will end with greatness.

4:26-29 — parable of the secretly growing seed.

4:30-32 — parable of the mustard seed.

4:33-34 — Mark explains Jesus' use of parables in teaching
the public.

Context of the Scriptures

1. Mark. Mark 4 contains three parables dealing with seed, and
also provides an explanatory conclusion which makes use of a similiar
metaphor. A review of the chapter provides us with the context of
the two parables for this Sunday.

4:1-20 — parable of the sower, seed, and soils (and an explanation.)

4:21-25 — observation that the truth cannot be kept secret.

4:26-29 — parable of the growing seed.

4:30-32 — parable of the mustard seed.

4:33-34 — Jesus' use of parables in teaching.

4:35-41 — Jesus' calming of a storm at sea.

2. Parallel passages: (Matthew 13:31-32; Luke 13:18-19) The
parallel passages deal only with the parable of the mustard seed. The
parable of the secretly growing seed appears *only* in Mark.

In Matthew's account of the mustard seed, the only difference
is in the fact that Matthew has the seed grow from a shrub into a
tree, while Mark does not mention a tree.

Luke's account is identical with Matthew's except that Luke does
not describe the mustard seed as the smallest of seeds, and does not
mention the shrub, only the tree. Whether the mustard seed grows
as large as a shrub or a tree has hermeneutical implications which
will be discussed later.

3. Related references to seed. The following references to seed
may be helpful in understanding the two parables to be dealt with
today:

Mark 4:1-20 — the parable of the sower, seed, and soils.

Mark 17:20 — At the foot of Mount Transfiguration, Jesus heals
an epileptic boy. The Disciples ask Jesus why they failed to heal him
while he was on top of the mountain. Jesus explains, "Because of
your little faith. For truly, I say to you, if you have faith as a grain
of *mustard seed,* you will say to this mountain, 'move hence to

yonder place,' and it will move; and nothing will be impossible to you" (author emphasis).

Luke 17:5 — The Disciples ask Jesus to increase their faith. He replies, "If you have faith as a grain of *mustard seed,* you could say to this sycamine tree, 'Be rooted up, and be planted in the sea,' and it would obey you" (author emphasis).

Matthew 13:24f — After good *seed* is sown, someone by night sows weeds (author emphasis).

John 12:24 — When Greeks come to see Jesus, he realizes that his end is near and interprets the occasion as his hour to be glorified. He comments, "Unless a *grain of wheat* falls into the earth and dies, it remains alone; but if it dies, it bears much fruit" (author emphasis).

1 Peter 1:23 — The new life in God results from imperishable seed. "You have been born anew, not of perishable *seed,* but of imperishable through the living and abiding Word of God" (author emphasis).

Content

Today's pericope (Mark 4:26-34) gives us two parables dealing with the Kingdom of God. The two have a common theme — i.e., growth of the Kingdom of God — but in the first (4:26-29) the growth is gradual, and in the second (4:30-32) growth is fantastic, growing from the smallest seed to a plant which is big enough to house the nests of birds. Although each parable alone may form the text and subject of a sermon, both parables may also be preached together because of the common theme. These short parables simply say that God causes his Kingdom to grow, and that it will not stop growing until it covers the world.

Precis (Mark 4:26-32)

Jesus taught that the Kingdom of God is like seed that is sown. The farmer, who sowed the seed, sleeps by night and lives day after day. He sees the seed growing but he cannot explain how it grows. The seed becomes a stalk, then a head appears, and finally the full grain in the head. When the grain is ripe, the farmer cuts it down, for the harvest has come. Jesus said again, "What shall we say the Kingdom of God is like or what parable can explain it? It is like

a mustard seed, the smallest of seeds, sown upon the ground. It grows
until it becomes the biggest of all shrubs. Its branches are so large
that birds make their nests in its shade."

Thesis: Like a seed, the Kingdom of God grows until it even-
tually covers the earth.
Theme: Great endings from tiny beginnings! or "Behold, what
God has wrought!"

Key Words in the Parable

1. **"Kingdom"** (vv. 26, 30) People living in a democracy may
have trouble with the word, "kingdom." In Jesus' day, every nation was a monarchy or dictatorship, and people could easily understand the concept of "kingdom." A kingdom is the realm of a
king who is the absolute ruler. The people in a kingdom belong to
the king and are obligated to obey and serve him. The Kingdom of
God is the realm of God, for he is absolute king, and in his realm
his commands are obeyed and his will is done. The citizens of the
Kingdom are the people of God. Where is God's kingdom located?
It is present in the believer and in the church, the fellowship of believers. The church is not the Kingdom of God, but the Kingdom
of God is in the church, even though it does not always obey the
King's commands or do his will. Because many do not understand
the Kingdom of God, Jesus gave these two parables to describe the
nature and work of the Kingdom.

2. **"Sleep"** (v. 27) After sowing the seed, the farmer in the parable went about his normal activities: sleeping at night and doing his
chores by day. Having sown the seed, he shows no anxiety about
the seed's productivity — he plants the seed in hope of an eventual
harvest, and has patience while the seed grows. "Sleep" reminds us
that the Kingdom of God comes from God and not from human
effort. The farmer does nothing but sow the seed. The parable does
not even mention his cultivating, fertilizing, or watering the seed,
and he does not even understand what or who causes the seed to
sprout. The arrival and establishment of the Kingdom of God on
earth is the work of God.

3. **"Harvest"** (v. 29) When the seed reaches maturity, in the

parable, it is harvested. There is, in other words, a productive completion of the growth process. The seed is not the victim of drought when only half grown, and cattle do not get into the field and tramp down the stalks, and hail does not break off the heads of grain. The point of the parable is that the Kingdom of God will not be curtailed or destroyed but will reach full maturity. Some interpret "harvest" eschatologically in terms of the final gathering of the nations and the separation of the sheep from the goats. But the parable is *not* referring to the End, but is simply saying that the seed will fulfill its destiny and produce fruit. Indeed, there *is* a harvest at time's end, but there is also an important harvest to be gathered now: "The harvest is plentiful, but the laborers are few." (Matthew 9:37)

4. "Like" (vv. 26, 30 [GNB]) "The kingdom of God is like this . . . " — like what? Is it like the seed that has the principle and power of life in it? Is it like the growth of the seed? Is it like the harvest that results from the seed? Could the kingdom of God be like all three of these?

5. "Smallest" (v. 31) Scholars tell us that the mustard seed is not really the smallest seed, but in Jesus' day it was by tradition the smallest seed. Be that as it may, the mustard seed is so small that the naked eye can barely see it. The point is that great things can come from the smallest beginnings. The Kingdom, after all, was started by a baby boy born in a barn and finally executed as a criminal on a shameful cross. The church began with eleven peasants who held no credentials other than the Holy Spirit. At the beginning, Christians were despised, persecuted, outlawed, and driven underground, and in the second century being a Christian was a crime in and of itself. Could a movement so small one day spread throughout of the world? Revelation answers us that evil will be conquered and destroyed and Jesus and his kingdom will triumph: "And he shall reign forever and ever."

6. "Sown" (vv. 31, 32) For the seed to grow and produce, it must first die and be buried. A seed cannot preserve itself by isolating itself from the soil, but it is only by dying that it achieves a new, fuller life as a plant with grain, fruit, or flower. To grow and produce, the Kingdom of God calls for the people in the Kingdom to die in order to gain a new life of productivity. This principle was enunciated by Jesus when he said, "Unless a grain of wheat falls into the earth and dies, it remains alone; but if it dies, it bears much fruit." (John 12:24) In the same manner, a disciple lives by the principle: "He who loves his life loses it, and he who hates his life in this world will keep it for eternal life." (John 12:25)

7. "Shrub" (v. 32) Only Mark says that the mustard seed grows into the greatest of shrubs, so great that birds use it for nests. Matthew and Luke both say that it grows into a tree. Since Mark is the earliest Gospel, his account is probably more authentic. The shrub is not a small plant, and it grows to be ten to twelve feet in height. The "tree," on the other hand, is sometimes understood eschatologically, so that it represents God's great Kingdom, and the birds in the tree stand for the nations of the world. Indeed, the day is coming when the kingdoms of the world will become the Kingdom of God, but this parable may not be teaching this. The parable simply depicts the contrast of the tiny seed, with its fabulous growth. The "tree" is also sometimes interpreted as a fulfillment of the prophecy found in Daniel 4:12 and Ezekiel 31:6.

Contemplation

With the context and content of the parables established, we find ourselves at the point where we should contemplate the truth, teachings, and principles in the parables for their possible proclamation this coming Sunday. This calls for musing, thinking, reflection, and meditating.

Insights

1. God's Doing. Contrary to much popular opinion, we do not bring nor establish God's Kingdom on Earth by our work, intelligence, and gifts. The Kingdom will be established on Earth by God. Jesus taught us to pray, "Thy kingdom come," for example, but if we brought the Kingdom, there would be no need to pray for God to send it. The parable of the secret growing seed calls attention to our helplessness in bringing the Kingdom to Earth. After sowing the seed, the farmer sleeps at night and leaves the growth of the seeds up to God, and when the seed sprouts, the farmer has no idea how it happened. The seed has an inherent power of life, and it is the Word of God which causes the Kingdom to grow. Our responsibility is to sow the Word, and to let it change our social order to one of peace and justice.

2. Hope. The parables teach us to hope. When the seed is sown, we can hope for a harvest, and when the mustard seed is sown, we can hope for a great shrub. When a farmer sows his seed, he can do no more than hope that God will send rain and sun for the seed to grow to maturity and harvest. It is easy for Christian workers to become discouraged because they cannot see any immediate results from their work. After preaching as deeply and passionately as possible, for example, a preacher often sees a congregation leaving, apparently unmoved. It is for this reason that preachers may often refer to "the foolishness of preaching." By teaching, preaching, and witnessing, however, we sow the seed of the Word in the hope that some day there will be a harvest. These parables give the preacher an opportunity to overcome discouragement in the church by giving all a sound basis for hope. The seed of God's Word will produce a harvest, and of this we can be certain!

3. Patience. "Rome was not built in a day." Nor does seed produce fruit in a day. Seed grows slowly to maturity. A mother's seed, for example, usually takes nine months for a baby to be born, while a farmer's seed demands that the farmer wait from spring to fall for the harvest. But modern people do not like to wait — we want instant tea or coffee, for the telephone to ring our party immediately, the TV and radio to begin performing without time for a warm-up. The Kingdom of God does not come overnight, however. The seed of the Word is sown and then we must patiently wait for results. This applies also to human relations: A sign on a pastor's desk said, "Be patient with me, for God is not finished with me yet." And parents need patience while the seed of their training produces the growth of good character in their children.

4. Potential. The parable suggests that great potential may come in tiny packages. What can a tiny mustard seed do, or amount to? In the seed is the power of life to grow to maturity, and in the parable the mustard seed becomes a shrub ten feet high. I was once asked an unforgettable question, when I was but a small boy, "Do you think you will ever amount to anything?'' There are also many old adages illustrating this theme: Big things come in small packages,'' "Out of an acorn comes a mighty oak,'' and "Despise not the day of small beginnings.'' And when in Bethlehem's barn a baby boy was born, who could have guessed that he would become the Savior of the world? A picture was taken of a human egg forty hours after conception and it was revealed to consist of only four cells no larger than the head of a pin. Here was a picture of a human being of microscopic size, and yet an adult human being has this tiny beginning. In the parable of the mustard seed, then, we have an unremarkable beginning but an amazing ending.

5. Victory. No matter how small the seed when planted, it will grow and produce a bountiful harvest. The Kingdom of God is coming and will cover the world: The day will come when the kingdoms of the world will join to become the Kingdom of God. Kings will die, nations will fall, beasts of evil will be destroyed, and the Kingdom of truth, love, justice, and peace will prevail. Like birds coming to a tree, the nations will seek refuge in God's Kingdom. This is the message of the book of Revelation, and this truth is implicit in today's parables.

6. Life out of death. When the pyramids of Egypt were explored, seed was found that was thousands of years old, but when planted, the seed produced wheat. Seed has life sealed inside, so that if it is put in a glass container, for example, the seed will preserve itself. In both parables in today's Gospel, however, the seed is sown — it's old identity dies and is buried. Out of this death grows a resurrection in the form of flowers or grain, and it is for this reason, for example, that flowers are usually placed on altars to signify the Resurrection. This process illustrates it is an eternal principle: no gain without pain, no success without work, no progress without sacrifice. Jesus compared his death to a seed buried in order to rise in new glory, and he taught that a life must be buried in his cause to be saved. It is not a question of a future life after death, but, rather, of life out of death in this world, in our time.

7. Growth. These parables deal with the growth of the Kingdom. In the first parable, the growth is gradual, from seed to stalk to ear to the full grain in the ear. In the second parable, there is remarkable growth from the smallest seed to the great shrub. In both parables then, we can see important characteristics of the Kingdom's growth:

A. Growth is certain — the seed sprouts without human effort.

B. Growth is secret — the farmer does not know how it grows.

C. Growth is gradual — from seed to harvest.

D. Growth is complete — it continues until the grain is mature.

Because of this growth, the Kingdom of God is here both now and in the future. At present, the Kingdom is not perfect nor universal — it is growing; at its consummation, the Kingdom will arrive in all of its bounty at the Parousia.

8. Secrecy. In the parable of the growing seed, the farmer "knows not how" the seed grows into a mature plant, since it is a mystery and one of God's secrets. What makes a seed germinate? Why does it grow? How is life contained in the tiny seed, and all the future form and product of the plant? How the Kingdom of God grows and produces a harvest of love, peace, joy, and justice is also a mystery. It is a mystery how God can create something out of nothing, or something great out of something of no apparent worth or size. It reminds us of Paul's words, "How inscrutable his ways! For who has known the mind of the Lord?" (Romans 11:34)

Homily Hints

1. The 3M of Growth. (4:26-29) The primary characteristic in both parables is growth: gradual growth to maturity, and fantastic growth to a big shrub. In the parable of the secretly growing seed we have —

A. The *miracle* of growth — v. 27

B. The *manner* of growth — v. 28

C. The *maturation* of growth — v. 29

2. God does it All! (4:26-32) Many people mistakenly believe that by our work and gifts to the church we are building the Kingdom and bringing it to Earth. The two parables, however, show that establishing the Kingdom on Earth is solely God's business.

A. God uses his people to —
1. Sow the seed of the Word — v. 26
2. Wait for the harvest — v. 28
3. Reap the harvest — v. 29
B. God provides the harvest —
1. Creates the seed
2. Causes the seed to grow — vv. 28, 32
3. Bring the seed to completion — harvest, shrub — vv. 29, 32

3. Hold Your Horses! (4:26-32) We want a better world right now, and we feel that we cannot afford to wait for world peace. The afflicted cry out for immediate justice: How long, O Lord, how long must we put up with crime, poverty, and ignorance? We want the Kingdom of God now, not after we are dead.

A. In our impatience, we take things into our own hands to bring the Kingdom to Earth:
1. Revolution — Zealots and violence
2. Pietism — Pharisees and rules of conduct
3. Legislation — Judaizers: "There ought to be a law against it."
4. Speculation — Apocalyptists: claim to know the hour of the Parousia.
B. Faith gives us patience to wait for the Kingdom to come Paul: "I am sure that he who began a good work in you will bring it to completion." (Philipians 1:6)
As the seed of the Word is planted in you, be patient — with social problems, with personal problems, with your spouse, children, and church.

Contact

How can these two parables in today's Gospel be applied to modern society? How can preachers interest the people in the lessons of these parables? Are we talking about which they could not care less, answering questions which they are not asking? Let us be honest and face the facts: How many in the average congregation are interested or concerned about the Kingdom of God? How many can even explain what is meant by "Kingdom"? Does it really matter to the congregation if the Kingdom grows or how it grows? If the parable of the mustard seed tells about the fantastic growth of the Kingdom, then how can we reconcile the parable with the huge numerical losses of American churches during the past decade? Do you think the people in the pews will "buy" the idea that a better world depends on God rather than on human efforts? These questions challenge a preacher to be realistic, relevant, and practical in preparing a sermon on today's parables.

Problems

As we begin our sermon preparation, we face certain problems which we need to be aware of so that we might handle them as best we can.

1. Kingdom. American congregations have difficulty in understanding the concept of the Kingdom of God since we have never lived in a kingdom. And because we are devotees of democracy, we may even have an antipathy toward the very idea of the kingdom. This may call for a careful explanation and defense of the term. Since the two parables tell us what the Kingdom of God is like, it is not possible to avoid the term altogether.

2. Bigness. Contemporary society is obsessed with bigness. We boast of belonging to the biggest church in town or in the denomination, or we may live in the biggest state in the union, or we may work for the biggest corporation. In contrast, the parables deal with the little seed that slowly grows into a harvest or great shrub. How can preachers, then, sell the idea of smallness when the public is so interested in bigness?

3. Urban society. The parables deal with an agricultural situation: soil, seed, harvest, farmer. They assume that we are familiar with these terms even though we live today in an industrial and technological age in which only 3% of the American population is living on a farm. How many members of your congregation, for example, farm for a living or even have a garden? These conditions present a challenge to the preacher to take the principles of the parables and translate them into terms meaningful to modern society.

Needs

Do these parables speak to the needs of the 20th-century people?

Consider the following:

1. Discouragement. Many Christians get discouraged in witnessing and performing good deeds because they cannot see any immediate results of their work. And this was precisely the occasion for Jesus' giving the parable of the secret growing seed. (4:26-29) For three years, Jesus and the Disciples preached, taught, and healed, but no progress could be seen — no change in society, no wholesale repentance, no mass revival. Even a pastor often feels discouraged when he/she sees no change in people's lives resulting from proclamation and pastoral care. Parents often feel the same way about the training of their children and take comfort in the saying, "Train up a child in the way he should go, and when he is old he will not depart from it." People today need to understand that the seed of the Word will grow and eventually produce results. We need that hope and assurance.

2. Smallness. In a society that glories in bigness, we need to appreciate the importance and the potential power of smallness. The parables stress the smallness of the seed and its eventual greatness and productivity. People need to know that a little faith can move giant mountains, that a little love can solve large problems, that a little word can give deep encouragement, that a little act can save the most desperately lost. God can make something special of a person of little or no apparent account, while a great institution may result from the dedication of one individual.

3. Humanism. We all know that we need a better world, since conditions in the world are so atrocious: civil rights are often disregarded, innocent people are tortured, the mad arms race may lead to cosmic destruction, many families are breaking up, sexual morality seems nonexistent. Who would believe us if we say, "Just sow the seed of the Word of God an all will be well"? Very few would agree. If the world is going to change for the better, we are going to have to get busy in changing it. So we are all in favor of social action, human rights, and the social gospel. But today's parables teach us that God's Kingdom of love, peace, and justice is God's work, so that our task is simply to sow the seed and allow God to give the increase. We must help our people to understand their proper role, no matter how difficult it is to communicate a message which seems to contradict our deepest feelings and best impulses.

Illustrative materials.

1. Seeing results. We often become discouraged because we see no results of our efforts. A bishop was the guest preacher in a certain church. At the time of the children's message, the children were allowed to ask the bishop about his work. One little fellow asked, "What do you like to do best?" He answered, "I like best to mow our lawn because I can see that I have done something."

2. Cooperation with God. God brings the Kingdom on Earth with the cooperation of humanity's sowing the seed and reaping the harvest. One day a man passed a garden full of flowers and vegetables. He called to the gardener, "What a beautiful garden God has given you!" "Yes," replied the gardener, "but you should have seen it when God had it alone."

3. Trying to do the impossible. Early one morning near the local high school football field, a pastor saw a large woodpecker fly to one of the steel poles. The woodpecker began to hammer his brains out against the side of the pole in hopes that he would get a bug or worm for his breakfast. The woodpecker never realized that it was a fruitless enterprise, for he kept at it for an hour. Trying to establish the Kingdom of God on Earth by human efforts is equally futile.

Augustine: "Without God we cannot; without us God will not."

H. Richard Niebur: "Man's task is not that of building utopias, but that of eliminating weeds and tilling the soil so that the Kingdom of God can grow. His method is not one of striving for perfection or of acting perfectly, but of clearing the road by repentance and forgiveness."

4. Patience during slow growth. For decades, Western missionaries preached almost fruitlessly to people of northern Nigeria. During this time the Nigerians wanted no religion but their own. Since the late 70s, the people of Nigeria have been turning to Christ by the hundreds so that today's missionaries ae desperately calling for help. 6000 Nigerians have joined the church, and 200 churches have been built. Hundreds have attended Bible training schools. The seed of the Word of God takes time to produce a bountiful harvest of souls.

5. Small beginnings and huge endings. the Rev. Mr. Wildmon, a Methodist pastor of a small church in Tupelo, Mississippi, began to protest against pornographic materials in the public media. He later founded the National Federation for Decency which grew from one to 350 chapters nationwide. One chapter in New England claims 1000 members and has picketed thirty adult magazine outlets in the region. One recent success was found in persuading Seven-Eleven stores to take *Playboy* and *Penthouse* magazines off the shelves.

6. Kingdom growth. "The last ten years has been the most dramatic harvest the world has ever seen," says Patrick Johnstone, research secretary of the Worldwide Evangelization Crusade. Since 1980, for example, 27,000 Chinese people have become Christians each day, and South Korea enjoys a 24% increase in church membership and has the world's largest churches. Costa Rica has had a 100% increase in four years, while in Argentina "people are falling all over each other to become Christians."

If the seed of the Word is causing God's Kingdom to grow so fantastically in some parts of the world, why is there a decrease in Western Europe and in America? In Finland, only 5% attend worship and a mere 1% take Communion. In Western Germany the average Lutheran church has 3000 members, but has a weekly attendance of only 100. And if the Church of Scotland continues to lose 19,000 members each year, she will cease to exist completly by 2030! In one year (1985) Methodists reported a loss of 65,000, Presbyterians 43,727, and Lutherans (LCA) 13,405. Is the western church failing to sow the seed of the kingdom?

7. Sow and sleep. Martin Luther once wrote, "I opposed indulgences and all the papists, but never with force. I simply taught, preached, and wrote God's Word, otherwise I did nothing. And while

I slept or drank Wittenberg beer with my friends Philip and Amsdorf, the Word so greatly weakened the papacy that no prince nor emperor ever afflicted such losses upon it. I did nothing: the Word did everything."

Proper 14 • Pentecost 12 • Ordinary Time 19

Common   Lutheran   Roman Catholic

6. Bread to Eat

John 6:35, 41-51

³⁵*Jesus said to them, "I am the bread of life; he who comes to me shall not hunger, and he who believes in me shall never thirst."*

⁴¹*The Jews then murmured at him, because he said, "I am the bread which came down from heaven." ⁴²They said, "Is not this Jesus, the son of Joseph, whose father and mother we know? How does he now say, 'I have come down from heaven'?" ⁴³Jesus answered them, "Do not murmur among yourselves. ⁴⁴No one can come to me unless the Father who sent me draws him; and I will raise him up at the last day. ⁴⁵It is written in the prophets, 'And they shall all be taught by God.' Every one who has heard and learned from the Father comes to me. ⁴⁶Not that any one has seen the Father except him who is from God; he has seen the Father. ⁴⁷Truly, truly, I say to you, he who believes has eternal life. ⁴⁸I am the bread of life. ⁴⁹Your fathers ate the manna in the wilderness, and they died. ⁵⁰This is the bread which comes down from heaven, that a man may eat of it and not die. ⁵¹I am the living bread which came down from heaven; if any one eats of this bread, he will live forever; and the bread which I shall give for the life of the world is my flesh."*

"Oh no, not for five Sundays!" a preacher may exclaim when he/she looks at the Gospel for Propers 12-16 (Pentecost 10-14). The Gospels deal with John 6 and with its single subject: bread. How can one deal creatively with the subject of bread for five sermons? Of these five passages, two are parables (or more accurately extended, metaphors) dealing with Jesus as the Bread of Life and with the eating of the bread of his flesh.

Bread is a familiar and important subject, however, which is certainly big enough for five Sundays. Physical bread is the universal staff of life. In the United States alone there are 19,000 bakeries employing over 350,000 people, and each year they mix eleven billion pounds of flour; 163 million pounds of dried milk, and 616 million pounds of shortening. The average American consumes about 70 pounds of bread annually. The top food sold in supermarkets is bread, and according to the *Progressive Grocer* magazine, 96.8% of shoppers buy bread, choosing from over 70 varieties.

Spiritual bread is even more important, however. The church's most vital task is to distribute living bread to every person in the world. This bread is so vital that Jesus even identified himself as "the bread of life." And, indeed, from his very birth he has been identified with bread, for he was born in Bethlehem, a word meaning "House of bread." Bethlehem was so named because it was situated in a good, fertile area which abounded in grain. And after his baptism, Jesus was asked to turn stones into bread. In his model prayer, furthermore, there is a petition for "daily bread," and to satisfy a hungry crowd, he provided bread for 5,000 and, later, for 4,000 — all from five loaves. When he instituted the Lord's Supper, he took bread, blessed and gave thanks for it, and said, "Take, eat. This is my body . . ." There must therefore be something terribly important about bread in order for it to get this amount of attention by Jesus, and also form the basis for a whole chapter in the book of John.

Context

Context of the Day

The subject of the Bread of Life does not constitute a unifying theme for this 12th Sunday after Pentecost (Proper 14). The First Lesson is one of a series of lessons on David's life. The Second Lesson is the fifth in a series of semi in-course readings from Ephesians. The Gospel is the third in a series of five passages from John 6. The Psalm of the Day is related to the First Lesson, and the Hymn deals with heavenly bread (Gospel). The Prayer offers a petition for mercy in terms of forgiveness and all good things. It is apparent that no clear or important unifying theme of the Lessons and Propers exists.

Context of the Lectionary

The First Lesson. (2 Samuel 18:1, 5, 9-15) Rebellious Absalom is killed in a war against his father, David.

The Second Lesson. (Ephesians 4:25—5:2) Since evil living grieves the Holy Spirit, we are to live in love as imitators of God.

Gospel. (John 6:35, 41-51) Today's Gospel needs to be seen in the perspective of the series of five readings from John 6.

John 6:1-15 (Proper 12, Pentecost 10) — Jesus provides bread for 5,000.
John 6:24-35 (Proper 13, Pentecost 11) — Jesus teaches that physical bread is insufficient for eternal life.
John 6:35, 41-51 (Proper 14, Pentecost 12) — Jesus says that he is the Bread of Life.
John 6:51-58 (Proper 15, Pentecost 13) — Jesus urges his followers to eat the Bread of Life for eternal life.
John 6:60-69 (Proper 16, Pentecost 14) — A divided response is given to Jesus' claim that he is the Bread of Life.

These five selections from John 6 constitute one unit with bread, both physical and spiritual as the unifying element. And unlike most other pericopes, these merge into each other. For instance, the last verse of the Gospel for Proper 13 (verse 35) is the first verse of the Gospel for Proper 14, and the last verse of the Gospel for Proper 14 is the first verse of Proper 15.

Context of the Scriptures

1. John. The book of John is concerned with the identity of Jesus as the divine Son of God. Today's passage, dealing with Jesus as the Bread of Life, is but one of a series of great "I am" passages.
I am living water — John 4.
I am the bread of life — John 6.
I am the light of the world — John 8.
I am the good shepherd — John 10.
I am the resurrection — John 11.
I am the vine — John 15.

Each passage is a facet in the diamond of the deity of Jesus. These facets do not compete with or contradict each other, but, rather, complement each other since each offers a related truth about the nature of Jesus.

2. Related Passages. Because Jesus as the Bread of Life is a metaphor found only in John, there are no parallel passages. Other references to bread in the Scriptures, however, may help to convey to us the important role and meaning of bread.

    A. God feeds his people —
        He feeds the Israelites with manna — Exodus 16:4
        Elijah is fed by ravens, (1 Kings 17:4) by a widow, (1
            Kings 17:9) and by an angel. (1 Kings 18:5)
    B. Bread is given to the enemy —
        Elisha feeds a conquered army — 2 Kings (6:20-23)
        Paul directs us to feed our enemy — Romans 12:20
    C. The horror of hunger is illustrated —
        Women eat their babies — 2 Kings 6:24-32.
    D. A case of poisoned food is shown — 2 Kings 4:38-41.
    E. The good news of bread is shared — 1 Kings 7:3-15
    F. The bread of Holy Communion is presented —
        Instituted by Christ — 1 Corinthians 11:23-26.
        The Church breaks bread — Acts 2:42
    G. The insufficiency of physical bread is noted —
        "Man shall not live by bread alone." — Matthew 4:4.
        "Why do you spend your money for that which is
         not bread?" — Isaiah 55:2.

Content

Precis (John 6:35, 41-51)

Jesus said to the people, "Because I am the Bread of Life, anyone who comes to me will not hunger and anyone who believes in me shall never thirst." The Jews took exception to his statement that he was the Bread that came from heaven. They reasoned: Is this Jesus not the son of Joseph? Do we not know his mother and father? How then can he say that he came from heaven? In response, Jesus told them not to complain, for no one can come to him unless God the Father draws him. The prophets say that God will teach all people, and everyone who knows the Father, and who has been taught by him, comes to Jesus. No one but Jesus has seen the Father. Everyone who believes in Jesus has eternal life. Jesus is the Bread of Life, not like the bread that came as manna in the wilderness. He who eats this manna will die, but Jesus is the living Bread from heaven that, if eaten, will grant life forever. And the bread Jesus gives to the world is his body.

Thesis: Jesus, the living bread from heaven, gives eternal life to believers.

Theme: The Bread of Life gives life!

Gospel: (John 6:35, 41-51)
> v. 35 — Jesus is the Bread of Life.
> v. 41 — The Bread of Life comes from heaven.
> v. 42 — The Jews object to Jesus' claim to deity.
> vv. 43-46 — Jesus gives his response: people who come to him are drawn by the Father.
> v. 47 — Believers in Jesus have eternal life.
> vv. 48-50 — Eat physical bread and you die; eat living bread and you live forever.
> v. 51 — The bread which gives life to the world is Jesus.

Key Words in the Parable

1. "Life." (v. 35) Jesus declares that he is the "bread of life." He was speaking to live people, however — they are alive whether or not they believe in him. But there is an important difference between "existence" and "life" — the one is physical and the other is spiritual. It is possible for people to exist without living, and to distinguish life from mere existence, the adjective "eternal" is used. Jesus is the bread of life, and this life is *real* life which consists of love, peace, and joy. This is a life of God, a life of oneness with Christ.

2. "Heaven." (vv. 41-42, 50-51) Jesus said that he is the bread of life that came from heaven. He was saying that he came from God and that he is God's Son — a claim of divinity. This was too much for the Jews to accept. After all, Christ was obviously a human being like one of them, and, moreover, they knew his origin — they knew his parents and where he lived. For a human to claim he is divine and that he is God's Son from heaven is to open himself to a charge of insanity.

This is not the only time when Jesus made this claim of heavenly origin. In John 4, Jesus told the Samaritan woman she was speaking to the Messiah. In John 9, Jesus told the man whose blindness he healed that he was looking at the Son of Man. The frequent claim of divinity aroused the hatred of several religious leaders. In John 10 we read, "The Jews answered him, 'We stone you for no good work but for blasphemy; because you, being a man, make yourself God.' " And when Pilate threatened to release Jesus, "the Jews answered him, 'We have a law, and by that law he ought to die, because he has made himself the Son of God.' " (John 19:7)

3. "Unless." (v. 44) Who can truly believe that Jesus came from heaven and is the Son of God? It is seemingly beyond human ability. But Jesus tells the Jews that no one can come to him "unless" drawn by God. We do not decide to come to Jesus, therefore, but he decides that we are his. We do not choose him — he chooses us as God calls, draws, and woos us through the Holy Spirit. There is no need, therefore, for an extended emotional appeal to persuade someone to be a Christian. We come to Christ because the Holy Spirit has persuaded us through the proclamation of the Word.

4. "Has." (v. 47) One who believes in Jesus as the bread from heaven "has" eternal life. "Has" is a verb in the present tense. This means that eternal life comes before physical death and not after: "*Today* you shall be with me in paradise." The moment we eat the Bread of Life is the moment eternal life begins. Heaven is a present reality.

5. "Living." (v. 51) Physical bread is said to be dead in contrast to the "living" bread of Christ, and it is true that physical bread soon dies — it gets hard, stale, and moldy. And a person who eats physical bread will also eventually die. Jesus claims to be "living bread" because he is of God and comes from God who is Life. Life gives life and Christ, therefore, is not a dead person who lived two millenia ago, but is forever living that he might give life to believers.

Contemplation

It is time now to reflect upon the parable of Jesus, the Bread of Life. What are the permanent values expressed in the passage? It is time to think quietly and privately so that we are open to the Spirit's guidance.

Insights

1. The necessity of bread. (6:48-51) We all acknowledge the fact that bread (food) is indispensible for life. This is true, however, both for physical and spiritual bread. Just as a physical body declines for lack of food to the point of death, so the soul disintegrates to the point of spiritual death. Since Christ is the Bread of Life, he is essential for a healthy, strong, and growing soul. The problem for many people lies in having a starved soul in an overfed body.

2. The source of bread. (6:41) Jesus says that the Bread of Life came from heaven as the manna once fell from the sky. Jesus is saying he is of God and from God. He claims to be the Son of God who came from heaven and who would return to heaven after his mission was completed on earth. This claim of divinity upset the religious leaders, because in their minds no human can dare to claim to be God. Because Christ is God's Son, he can feed the soul and grant eternal life, but this first calls for faith that he is indeed the Bread from heaven. (v. 35)

3. Living Bread. (6:51) Jesus also says that he is "the living bread," and this suggests two things. First, Jesus is living now and forever — he is not a dead person belonging to ancient history; because of his resurrection, he lives as much today as when he lived in Nazareth. In Revelation, the risen Bread of Life says, "Fear not, I am the first and the last, and the living one; I died, and behold I am alive forevermore . . . " (1:17-18) Indeed, we today pray to a living Christ, worship a living Redeemer, and serve a living Savior. Second, because Christ is the living bread, he and his Bread can make people come alive. When on Earth, his touch brought a young man to physical life; today, contact with him brings spiritual life.

4. Life in the present. (6:47) In today's pericope, eternal life is frequently mentioned: "I will raise him up at the last day," "he who believes has eternal life," "a man may eat of it and not die," and "If any one eats of this bread, he will live forever." This eternal life begins here and now at the time one first believes that Jesus is the Bread of Life. It is a special quality of life, this life in Christ. This "high quality" life consists of love, truth, joy, and peace. Contrary to popular opinion, eternal life for a Christian does not begin at physical death, but before death — e.g., Paul assures us in Romans 8 that the life we have in Christ cannot be destroyed by death.

5. Bread for growth. In a time when many Protestant churches are concerned about declining membership, it needs to be pointed out that the Bread of Life can lead to church growth. It is, after all, common knowledge that hungry people go where they can get food; that an empty bird feeder brings no birds to your house; that you can usually tell a restaurant's quality of food by the crowded parking lot and the long line of hungry customers waiting to be seated and served. Likewise, people will come to the church where their spiritual hunger is met, where the Bread of Life is proclaimed and dispensed. Moreover, when people are fed and are excited about the food received, they automatically tell others where they too can get good food for their souls.

6. The Divine Call. (6:42-46) The question is often asked, "How can we get people to become Christians?" We often invite, beg, and plead for people to come to Christ, to accept him as Lord and Savior. Some belive an "altar call" should be made at the close of each worship service. Occasionally, evangelists in revivals put undue pressure and often manipulate people by putting on emotional pressure to get people to the "altar" to make a confession. According to today's Gospel Jesus would have no part of any of these pleas. He says that no one can choose to come to God on his own volition or strength, for God alone draws a person to believe. When a person knows God, he/she will acknowledge Christ as God's Son and will see God in him. We do not choose Christ, but Christ chooses us. How does Christ choose us? When the Word is preached, and people hear and accept the Word, the Holy Spirit calls, enlightens, and gathers a person into the Kingdom. Our responsibility is to preach the Word clearly and dynamically so that God through the Holy Spirit will cause a person to respond in faith.

Homily Hints

1. Life Before and After Death. (6:47) True life in eternal life — begins with life in Christ. It is an immediate possession which is held forever. The only difference between life in Christ on earth and life in Christ in heaven is that the latter is fuller, greater, and more abundant.

To have life before and after death —
   A. Know Jesus as the Bread of Life — v. 48
   B. Believe in Jesus as the Bread of Life — v. 47
   C. Eat the Bread of Life — v. 51

2. Speak for Yourself, Jesus! (6:41-51) For every generation and with each person the question which presents itself is, "Who is Jesus?" But Jesus is never what any other person thinks or says he is, whether the person is a philospher, theologian, scholar, prophet, Christian, or non-Christian. Only Jesus knows himself, and in this passage he tells us who he is.
   A. "I am the bread of life" — vv. 35, 38
   B. "I came from heaven" — vv. 41, 42
   C. "I am the living bread" — v. 51

3. "I Can't Live Without You!" — (6:35, 50-51) A person in love with another often claims, "I can't live without you." A Christian might very well say that to Jesus. Just as no one can live physically without food, so Christ is our spiritual food, and the soul cannot live without his nourishment.
   With Christ as our Bread, we can truly live because —
   A. Christ the Bread eternally satisifies our hunger — v. 35
   B. Christ the Bread gives himself to us — v. 51
   C. Christ the Bread supplies us with eternal life — vv. 50, 51

4. Soul Food. "I am the bread of life." — v. 48. Christ is spiritual bread for the soul. Just as the physical body needs food to live, so the soul needs nourishment. He is, therefore, the most important kind of "soul food." Having been fed with the Bread of Life, a person can sing, "All is well with my soul. It is healthy, robust, and strong." Some will ask, "How does Christ feed my soul?"

A. Christ feeds us with the bread of God's promises.

B. Christ feeds us with the bread of his love.

C. Christ feeds us with the bread of the Spirit's presence.

5. Modern Manna. (6:41-42, 50) When the Israelites were in the wilderness without food for forty years, God provided it by sending manna. Similarly, God now sends a more vital manna for the feeding of the souls of the people. This manna is Christ, the Bread of Life. Jesus' statement that he came from heaven caused the religious leaders of his day to object strenuously, for they could see only a human being in Jesus.

Because Christ the Bread of Life came from heaven —

A. The Bread is imperishable.

B. The Bread is inexhaustable.

C. The Bread is evidence of God's grace.

D. The Bread is nourishing.

Contact

Problems

1. According to the Lectionary, a preacher faces the problem of dealing with bread for five consecutive Sundays. The problem is further complicated by the fact that we have two parables for this and for next Sunday. How can we avoid repetition over these five Sundays? Might the subject be exhausted after one sermon alone? Can we find sufficient illustrative material to vary the theme's presentation for five Sundays?

The two "bread" parables each emphasize different elements of our relationship with Christ, however. In Proper 14, the focus is upon the identity of Jesus as the Bread of Life, and what that means both to him and to us. The following Sunday, on the other hand, we will deal with the acceptance and digestion of this Bread into our lives. Bread, after all, is to be eaten and not merely to be admired or revered. Bread must be taken into ourselves so that the food can strengthen and refresh us. On the first Sunday, then, we look at the Bread for what it is; on the second Sunday we are to eat the Bread.

2. There is a craving in our world for physical bread, but a neglect of spiritual bread. Jesus himself faced this problem after he fed the 5000: When they returned to him on the other side of the sea, he said to them, "You seek me, not because you saw signs but because you ate your fill of the loaves. Do not labor for the food which perishes, but for the food which endures to eternal life." (John 6:26, 27)

How can we persuade people to desire spiritual bread as intensely as they seem to want physical bread? How can we get them to pray for spiritual bread as often as they pray for daily bread in the Lord's Prayer? If only people would crave spiritual bread as strongly as they pled to have stones changed into bread for their mouths and stomachs. We all feel the pangs of physical hunger, but are there no similar pangs of spiritual hunger?

Points of Contact

1. Every person is somehow connected with bread, the symbol of food. Indeed, it is often an instance of one of two extremes: On the one hand, bread is a problem for people who eat too much — e.g., obesity, the physical problems connected with overeating, and the billions of dollars spent annually for various kinds of diets and for exercise in health spas; on the other hand, the lack of bread causes malnutrition or even starvation. The world is aware of millions who are starving and both churches and secular organizations appeal for funds to send food to the hungry — e.g., "Food for the Hungry" or "Bread for the World."

But is there the same concern for the billions of people who are starving for the lack of the Bread of Life?

2. Bread is a familiar element in the life of every person. It does not matter how rich or poor one may be, for Bread in some form is served at every meal — e.g., crackers, rolls, biscuits, muffins, cereal, and so forth. It is a challenge for a preacher to take this most common element and translate it into a more spiritual reality. What does it mean to say Jesus is the Bread of Life? How does one eat this heavenly bread?

Illustrative Materials

Hunger.

450,000 people in the world today are hungry. 40,000 children under age five die of malnutrition every day — a total of fifteen million each year. In Africa 150 million people faced starvation because of the drought in 1984. While the USA has 60% of the world's food reserves, the US Governnment gave only 25% of the amount needed to prevent wholesale starvation.

———

In a supermarket, a senior citizen found her bill was eighteen cents more than she had. She asked the clerk at the checkout counter to remove a can of cat food from her order. The clerk offered to pay for it because "I don't want your cat to go hungry." The old lady replied with a weak smile, "I am the cat."

Bread for the World

It seems that every region of Earth has its own particular kind of bread: the rye of Germany, the shortbread of Scotland, the scone of England, the tortilla of Mexico, the cornbread of America, and the croissant of France. But there is only one bread for the whole world — Jesus, the Bread of Life.

Proper 15 • Pentecost 13 • Ordinary Time 20

Common   Lutheran   Roman Catholic

---

8. Eat the Bread

John 6:51-58

---

[51] *"I am the living bread which came down from heaven; if any one eats of this bread, he will live for ever; and the bread which I shall give for life of the world is my flesh."* [52] *The Jews then disputed among themselves, saying, "How can this man give us his flesh to eat?"* [53] *So Jesus said to them, "Truly, truly, I say to you, unless you eat the flesh of the Son of man and drink his blood, you have no life in you;* [54] *he who eats my flesh and drinks my blood has eternal life, and I will raise him up at the last day.* [55] *For my flesh is food indeed, and my blood is drink indeed.* [56] *He who eats my flesh and drinks my blood abides in me, and I in him.* [57] *As the living Father sent me, and I live because of the Father, so he who eats me will live because of me.* [58] *This is the bread which came down from heaven, not such as the fathers ate and died; he who eats this bread will live for ever."*

Eat to live or live to eat? We can eat to our salvation or damnation. At the beginning of the human race, eating led us into sin, separation from God, and judgment; in the end, we are promised that we shall eat from the tree of life in the presence of God who will eat with us. It is not, in other words, merely a matter *that* we eat, but *what* we eat. To live physically we must have bread (food) lest we die of malnutrition, but to live spiritually we must have the Bread of Life, which is Jesus, the Son of God, who gives himself to the world as spiritual food.

In America, thank God, we have plenty of physical food. By his/her 70th birthday, the average American consumes fourteen steers, twenty-five hogs, three-and-a-half lambs, and 1050 chickens. Each year the average American eats seventy pounds of bread. But to what extent does the average American eat the Bread of Life? Are we physically well fed but spiritually malnourished? Today's "parable" urges us to eat the spiritual food to be found only in Jesus Christ.

Context

Context of the Day

The Day is Proper 15. It is an ordinary day of the Pentecost season, and has no special event or doctrine to celebrate. Similiar to last Sunday, there is no unifying theme of Lessons and Propers. The First Lesson continues the story of David's life. The Second Lesson constitutes another reading from Ephesians. The Gospel for the Day is the fourth lesson from John 6. And as usual, the Psalm refers to the First Lesson; it is a lament by someone who experiences distress, and David could well have written it because of his grief over the death of his son, Absalom. However, the Psalm is also related to the Gospel and the subject of bread: "For I eat ashes like bread." (v. 9) and "I forgot to eat my bread." (v. 4) The Prayer of the Day can be applied to the Gospel:

1. One of the "precious promises" is eternal life;

2. "Perfect faith," for which we pray, is needed to believe that eating Jesus as the Bread of Life will produce eternal life.

Context of the Lectionary

The First Lesson. (2 Samuel 18:24-33) David weeps over the news that his son, Absalom, was killed.

The Second Lesson. (Ephesians 5:15-20) Because the days are evil, Christians walk wisely by making most of the times.

Gospel. (John 6:51-58) Eating the flesh and drinking the blood of Jesus leads to eternal life. The Gospels for today, and for last Sunday, are two of a series of five lessons dealing with bread. Last Sunday, Jesus identified himself as the Bread of Life, while today's Gospel would have us partake of this heavenly bread. It is one thing to have bread and quite another to eat it. The supply of "living bread" is adequate for all people, but unless it is eaten, people will spiritually die. Consequently, the two Gospels are dealing with the same subject: identification and consumption of the Bread of Life.

Last Sunday we found the Bread; this Sunday we are to eat it for eternal life.

Another connection between today's and last Sunday's Gospel is that both contain controversy over Jesus' message. Last Sunday the people were upset over Jesus' claim that he came down from heaven like the manna of old; the pople are again critical of his saying that they who eat his flesh and drink his blood have eternal life.

Context of the Scriptures

The "bread" of John 6 needs to be seen in the perspective of the Scriptures since even a cursory survey indicates that the bread of John 6 is not an isolated or independent subject.

1. Eve and Adam eat the food of disobedience. Genesis 2:17, 3:6; and compare Revelation 2:7.
2. Upon Abraham's request, Sarah bakes bread to serve to visiting men of God. Genesis 18:1-8
3. Esau sells his birthright for a dish of food. Genesis 25:29-34
4. The passover meal is eaten with unleavened bread. Exodus 12:15-20
5. Yahweh feeds the Israelites in the wilderness with manna. Exodus 12:15-20
6. Bread is offered to Yahweh. Exodus 25:23-30. ("On the table there is always to be the sacred bread offered to me.") Compare: God in Jesus offers bread to the world. John 6:41.
7. Having no food, David eats sacred bread. 1 Samuel 21:1-6.
8. Taste the food: "O taste and see that the Lord is good." (Psalm 34:8) Compare: "You have tasted the kindness of the Lord." 1 Peter 2:3.
9. Eat the Word and then speak. Ezekiel 3:1-3; Revelation 10:8-11.
10. Hunger for food tempts Jesus to turn stones into bread. Matthew 4:1-3.
11. Jesus provides bread for 5,000. Matthew 14:13-21.
12. People who refused to eat. Luke 14:15-24.
13. Jesus warns against the yeast of the Pharisees (poisoned bread!). Matthew 16:5-11.
14. Jesus institutes the Lord's Supper. 1 Corinthians 11:23-24.
15. Jesus reveals himself in the breaking of bread at Emmaus. Luke 24:28-32.

16. Jesus serves bread at an Easter breakfast. John 21:7-13
17. Should Christians eat meat sacrificed to idols? 1 Corinthians 8:1-6
18. What happens when God comes to eat with us? Revelation 3:20

Context of the Hymnal

Hymns dealing with the Bread of Life can suggest preaching themes. The Hymn of the Day, "How Blest Are They Who Hear God's Word," reminds us that the Bread of Life can be eaten through the preached Word. It is similar to "Break Thou the Bread of Life." "O Living Bread from Heaven" reminds us that Jesus is the living bread. "For the Bread Which You have Broken" leads us to be thankful. "Here, O my Lord, I see Thee Face to Face" helps us realize that in eating the bread of Communion we enter into a mystical union with Christ. To invite and encourage us to eat the Bread of Life we may sing, "Draw Near and Take the Body of the Lord," or "Let us Break Bread Together on our Knees." Then we come to the Table of the Lord with a humble prayer: "Lord Jesus Christ, We Humbly Pray." A review of the hymns dealing with the Word and Eucharist will not only suggest subjects for sermons, but will also put us in the proper mood and spirit for eating the Bread of Life.

Content

Precis (John 6:51-58)

Jesus is speaking to the people assembled in the synagogue at Capernaum: "I am the living bread that came from heaven. If anyone eats this bread, he will always live. The bread is my flesh which I give to the world that it may live." This upset many people who angrily asked, "How can he give us his flesh to eat?" To this Jesus answered, "To tell you the truth, if you do not eat my flesh and drink my blood, you will not have life in you. Anyone who eats my flesh and drinks my blood has eternal life and will be raised on the last day. For my flesh is real food and my blood is real drink. Whoever eats my flesh and drinks my blood lives in me and I in him. Just as the living Father God sent me and I live in him, one who eats me will live because of me. I am the bread which came down from heaven, not like the bread the ancient Israelites ate and then died, but the bread that causes one to live forever."

Thesis: By eating Jesus one has eternal life.

Theme: Eat and Live!

Gospel: Today's Gospel is a continuation of last Sunday's Gospel. The connecting link is verse 51 which ends last Sunday's Gospel and begins today's Gospel. Last Sunday's Gospel told us that Jesus is the Bread of Life that came from heaven. In today's Gospel the emphasis is upon eating this Bread of Life. If Jesus is the Bread of Life, then to eat it is to eat Jesus' flesh. This causes an irate protest of on the part of the assembled congregation at Capernaum as they objected to the idea that this man from Nazareth taught that eternal life depended upon eating his flesh.

> 6:51 — Jesus is the living bread from heaven which, if eaten, gives eternal life.
>
> 6:52 — Many people object to the idea of eating Jesus' flesh.
>
> 6:53-55 — To eat his flesh is to have eternal life; not to eat it means no true life.
>
> 6:56 — Jesus lives in the person who eats this Bread.
>
> 6:57 — As Jesus lives because of his Father, a person who eats Jesus also lives.
>
> 6:58 — Eat only physical bread and you die; eat the Bread of Life and you live forever.

Key Words in the Parable

1. "Bread." (vv. 51, 55) Jesus repeatedly refers to himself as the Bread of Life. It is an appropriate term, for bread is a basic staple of the food on which one physically lives. As used here, however, bread is meant to mean more than rolls, biscuits, muffins, or croissants. In verse 55, Jesus says, "My flesh is food indeed." Bread is food, the entire meal, and thus Jesus is not merely one of many different types of food. Jesus is food for the soul and, as such, he is indispensible and essential for life. What kind of bread is he — "living" (v. 51), "from heaven; (divine) and unleavened (sinless)?

2. "If." (v. 51) This living bread of Jesus must be eaten: *"If* any one eats this bread . . ." We usually eat because we are hungry. We may crave food and say, "I am so hungry I could eat a horse and chase the rider." A meal may be bounteous, but without an appetite we can only look at it and walk away. Food is meant to be eaten — just as a song is not a song until it is sung and a bell is not a bell until it is rung. And because of hunger pains we become ravenous. Our problem is that we do not have *spiritual* hunger pains — or do we? Is prayer a spiritual hunger pain? Do alcohol and drugs indicate that we are spiritually hungry for true life? Are people going to various cults and sects because their spiritual hunger is not being met by mainline churches? Many people are spiritually hungry, in other words, but they are unconscious of it. If only God had given us spiritual hunger pains as obvious as our physical hunger pain!

Moreover, The Bread of Life must be desired because this kind of bread cannot be purchased at any price, or even earned. It is a pure gift of grace — "the bread which I shall *give.* " (v. 51) To receive the gift of Bread, one must first desire it and ask for it, and then accept it by faith. At the Last Supper, Jesus said, "Take, eat." There needs to be a human response when Jesus offers his body for eating. We will take it *if* we are hungry for him.

3. **"Eat."** (v. 51 et al.) "Eat" occurs eight times in this short pericope. We are to eat the Bread and thereby consume the flesh of Jesus. To eat means to take a personal experience of Christ into our lives as we take physical food into our stomachs. We receive him and join him to us so that we become one with him. A loving parent says to a small child, "You are so sweet. I think I'll eat you up!", and when we want a child's kiss, we say, "Give me some sugar." This is similar to what we mean by eating Jesus, the Bread. Christ thereby becomes personal, concrete, and physical. According to the Revised Standard Version, Psalm 34:8 says, "O taste and see that the Lord is good!" The Good News Bible translates this as "Find out for yourself how good the Lord is." Peter writes to his people, "You have tasted the kindness of the Lord." (1 Peter 2:3)

4. **"Flesh."** (vv. 51-56) The word "flesh" also occurs frequently in this passage — at least six times. What exactly is it that we are to eat? If it is simply bread, there is no problem. But Jesus says we are to eat his flesh. Since John does not give an account of the Last

Supper, some scholars believe this passage is in lieu of the institution of Holy Communion when Jesus invites his Disciples to eat his body and drink his blood in the forms of bread and wine. How shall we understand this? Literally — in terms of transubstantiation? Symbolically — in terms of bread and wine as representatives of his body and blood? Or could it be both: the real presence of Jesus and the actual bread and wine? In next Sunday's Gospel, Jesus explains what he meant when he said that we are to eat his flesh: "It is the spirit that gives life, the flesh is of no avail." (John 6:63) Can the spiritual presence of Jesus become identified with the material? It clearly did so in the Incarnation: "The Word became flesh . . . " (John 1:14) The Holy Spirit comes into the physical bodies of believers, and the real spiritual presence of Christ can and does present itself in the forms of bread and wine. Through them, Christ comes into us as we eat and drink in faith.

5. **"How?"** (v. 52) As did the people in Jesus' day who heard these words for the first time, we also ask, "How can this man give his flesh to eat?" How is it possible for the bread to be bread and yet also be the flesh of Jesus? How can the wine of Communion also be the blood of Jesus? We must admit that we do not know the answers to these questions. It is a mystery of our faith. Yet we accept and use many things we do not understand and cannot explain. Do you understand how a microwave oven heats food without getting hot? Can you explain how a computer figures and remembers? Though we cannot explain it, we still experience the real presence of Jesus when we eat the bread of his flesh and drink the wine of his blood.

6. **"Abides."** (v. 56) In the Mystery Religions, eating the flesh of an animal sacrificed to a god was to also eat the god — to take the god inside you. In this way pagans believed they were "god-filled." In a similiar way, when we eat Jesus' flesh and drink his blood, he abides in us and we in him. As food is assimiliated and then identified with the body, so Christ and the believer become one: there is a mystical union of Christ and the believer. This is what Paul meant by the phrase, "in Christ" — i.e., by taking Christ into us by eating him, we abide, remain, continue in him. It is a glorious, intimate, and personal union. We are then Christ-centered and Christ-saturated people.

Contemplation

What is there to proclaim in this Gospel lesson that was not proclaimed last Sunday on the subject of the Bread of Life? Last Sunday the focus was on Jesus as the Bread of Life, but today we look at the actual eating of the Bread for eternal life and salvation.

Insights

1. Fellowship of Food. (6:53-57) There is more to a meal than food, and in fact, food may be secondary to the fellowship formed around the table. We usually eat with another person because the guest was invited — e.g., as Jesus said, "Take and eat." It is a token of grace and goodwill to be invited to eat with others. Moreover, eating with others also signifies equality and acceptance, and for this reason Jesus was criticized for eating with sinners, for it implied his approval. In Joseph's day, his brothers had to eat by themselves, because Egyptians refused to eat with Hebrews. (Genesis 43:32) In past years many American whites did not eat with blacks. A meal also means fellowship — a sharing of thoughts and feelings. It indicates friendship, love, and respect. A meal may even be a means of reconciliation — as it was when Jesus prepared an Easter breakfast by the Sea of Galilee to reconcile and reunite his Disciples.

2. Necessity of Eating. (6:53-56) Some people live only to eat and they can easily become obese. In contrast, good Christians are to eat to live. Without physical food we cannot live physically, but a human is more than a body since each also has a soul that needs its own nourishment for life and strength. The supply of bread for the soul is Christ, and he is adequate and sufficient for every soul. We can be physically fat and yet at the same time spiritually "skinny." Before we can willingly eat, we first need to be hungry. Are we spiritually hungry and yet not know that we are? Do we feel that something is wrong, but not see that we need Christ within us? How then can we get Christ in us? The answer is given us today: we are to eat him and drink his blood. By so eating him we may possess him so that he will dwell in our minds and hearts.

3. Ways of Feeding The Soul. (6:52) The people asked, "How can this man give us his flesh to eat?" How can we feed our souls with Jesus? Jesus is the food for our souls because that food is in the Word of God and Jesus is the Word that became flesh when he was on Earth. While he is in heaven, the Word is in the Scriptures, and when we read them, therefore, we feed our souls. When the Word is proclaimed in classroom or in pulpit, the Word feeds the souls of listeners; when the Word is offered in the Sacraments, then the recipients of Baptism and Holy Communion are fed with the Bread of Life. In each case, we are eating the Bread of Life for the strengthening and the very life of our souls.

4. Times of Eating. In the Gospel today, there is no mention of how often we are to partake of the Bread of Life. Are we to conclude that we need eat only once in a lifetime, or is it meant to be a daily experience? We eat physical food three times a day and if we only miss one meal we feel abused. Does not the soul need the same constant nourishment as the body does? There is to be a daily eating of Bread by Bible reading, and the soul can also be fed weekly when we worship and receive the Word orally. Many churches provide the sacramental meal on a monthly basis and the trend in some Denominations is to celebrate the Holy Communion each week. Feeding the soul is indeed a *daily* necessity if we are to grow into the fullness of the stature of Christ.

5. Thanks for the Meal. Today's pericope is related to the institution of the Lord's Supper. Since the Upper Room experience, the church has eaten the flesh and drunk the blood of Jesus through the Holy Communion. This is known also as the Eucharist, a Greek word for "Thanksgiving," and therefore, the consecration of the elements is called "The Great Thanksgiving." When a meal is over, courtesy demands that the guests thank the host and/or hostess, and for the heavenly feast, we are similarly grateful — for the spiritual food, for the fellowship and oneness with Christ, for the forgiveness and reconciliation, and for the presence of Christ himself.

6. This is the Life. (6:51, 54, 58) Life is a main theme of today's Gospel as Jesus urges us to eat in order to live. This calls, however, for eating the right food. Eat only physical food and eventually you will die but also eat the spiritual food which is Christ, the Bread of Life, and you will live forever. In this passage the emphasis is on spiritual life, not physical. This bread is a "living bread" because

Christ is life itself. Jesus referred to his "living Father," for God is life, and people who eat the heavenly bread receive eternal life now. This is what Christianity is all about: life. Jesus said he came that we might have life. Death is humanity's greatest enemy: not physical death which is natural, but the spiritual death which is separation from God. This is life — to know, to believe in, to accept, and to serve Christ.

Homily Hints

1. **Holy Hunger.** (6:51, 58) How shall the spiritually hungry be satisfied? It is the business of the church to spiritually feed people. This can be done — only under the following conditions:
   A. People must be hungry — "If" (v. 51)
   B. Bread must be available — "I am the living bread" (v. 51)
   C. Bread must be distributed — Word and Sacraments
   D. Bread must be eaten — "Unless you eat" (v. 53)

2. **Hunger of the Heart.** (6:51, 53) Unless we are hungry, we will not eat. Are people hungry for Christ — for the life he alone can give? Are we trying to satisfy a hunger we do not understand by indulging in drugs, alcohol, sex, and cults? We may feel lonely, unfulfilled, and isolated. Something is lacking in life and we are hungry for the fullness of life. We need to recognize the hungers of our hearts —
   A. Hunger for help through prayer
   B. Hunger for God's presence — Psalm 42:1-2
   C. Hunger for forgiveness

3. **Why eat?** (6:51-58) Why do we eat? Merely because it is meal time? Because it is a habit? Because we receive an invitation to dinner? Christians, on the other hand, have very good reasons for eating the Bread of Life —
   A. Eat for food (spiritual) — v. 55
   B. Eat to live — v. 54
   C. Eat to be one in Christ — v. 56

4. **You Can Live Forever!** (6:51-58) No one really wants to die. There is a force in all creation to live, and we struggle against every obstacle in order to live. Several times in this passage we are told

that we can live forever —
    A. We eat "living bread" — vv. 51, 54
    B. We have a "living Father" — v. 57

Contact

Problems

1. The commonality of bread. Bread is so commonplace — almost everyone eats bread at least daily. This can be a problem for preachers. How can anyone say something new, different, or creative about bread? Preaching this Sunday's parable demands a special creativity.

2. Controversy. The subject of bread and its relationship to Holy Communion is controversial today, and it was also in Jesus' day. When he spoke of himself as bread from heaven, many of his listeners were critical and offended as he appeared to be a human being just as they were. Later he called upon them to eat his flesh and this aroused even more opposition and angry disagreement, since it sounded like cannibalism. The Holy Communion, in which we eat his flesh as bread and drink his blood as wine, is still a sore subject of controversy in the church. We can agree on many doctrines: we can support practical programs of service, but we still refuse to commune together. At the last convention of the World Council of Churches, for example, one denomination separated from the others to have its own service of the Eucharist. Lutherans agree with Roman Catholics on the doctrine of justification, but are not as yet allowed to commune at Roman altars. In dealing with today's Gospel lesson, therefore, we need to be aware of its controversial nature in today's churches.

3. Interpretation. Another problem presented by today's "parable" is the interpretation of "flesh" and "blood." Is it to be taken literally or figuratively? The people in Jesus' day took his words literally, so when he invited them to drink his blood, he was violating the Jewish prohibition of drinking the blood of animals or of humans. In Leviticus 17:14 blooddrinking is forbidden: "For the life of every creature is the blood of it; therefore I have said to the people of Israel, You shall not eat the blood of any creature, for the life of every creature is its blood." Blood is considered the life of the creature. To drink blood is to take the life of another person into oneself. Later, Jesus explained he was speaking figuratively about his body and blood: "It is the spirit that gives life, the flesh is of no avail; the words that I have spoken to you are spirit and life." (John 6:63) Before preaching on this pericope, a preacher needs to come to an understanding of the meaning of the text.

4. More than bread. There is a tendency to understand the Bread of Life as only bread, as one item of a meal. However, it needs to be made clear that "bread" represents the entire meal. We need no food other than Jesus since he alone can feed the soul. As the Bread of Life, Jesus is the Word made flesh, the incarnate Word. As bread, the Word is served in several ways: in proclamation, the Bread of Life is broken and distributed to hearers; in literature (the Bible) the Word as Bread is eaten by readers; and the Word is eaten and received visibly in the Sacraments. The physical bread of the Eucharist is the Bread of Life, while the Word is spiritual food for hungry people.

Points of Contact

What connection is there between modern people and the eating of sacramental bread? Where is the relevance? Are we talking about something that is a part of people's lives?

1. It is one thing to have bread and another to eat it. People know of Jesus as the Bread of Life, but how many have "eaten" him, really taken him into their lives to the point that they are "in Christ" and Christ in them? For some, Christianity is a formal, external matter taken as a matter of tradition, custom, or habit. Today's Gospel reading calls for a personal and intimate union with Christ.

2. The quality of life is more important to people than its mere quantity. The pericope frequently mentions that eternal life comes by eating the Bread of Life. The quality of life is also expressed in "eternal," however, because it is life of God and Christ that has no ending, for God is life and cannot die. In this "parable" then, we are dealing with a fundamental need and desire of people. In spite

of this, in the average Protestant church in America approximately 40% of the members neglect the reception of Holy Communion year after year.

3. This passage is considered to be John's version of the Last Supper. It is related to Holy Communion when the faithful eat Jesus' flesh and drink his blood in the forms of bread and wine. The subject of Communion is still discussed in today's church. Questions like these are being discussed:

Should infants be given Communion?
Should children before Confirmation receive the Eucharist?
Should the Lord's Supper be administered every Sunday?
Should lay persons be permitted to administer the elements?
Should the common cup be used in the light of AIDS?

Illustrative Materials

1. **Daily Bread.** The commander of a local army post received a complaint from one of the soldiers about the bread being served. The commander snapped back at him angrily, "If Napoleon had had that bread in Russia, he would have eaten it with the greatest delight." "Yes, sir," replied the soldier, "but it was fresh then."

Jesus has us pray for "daily" bread. A fresh supply of manna was sent to the Israelites every day except on the Sabbath. Spiritual food is needed daily.

2. **Who feeds your soul?** An obese student was confronted by his professor for his low grades. In the course of the conversation, the professor remarked, "If you would feed your mind like you feed your body, your grades would be better." The student replied, "Yes sir, but you feed my mind and I feed my body."

3. **Bread of consolation.** A pastor tells about his mother's custom of going to a bereaved family with a loaf of homemade bread and a hug. Later, when the family felt like talking, she went back to listen to their expression of grief.

4. **Problem of distribution.** Not every country is capable of feeding itself. In the United States we produce enough food to feed over a billion people, yet 25 million Americans are hungry. One tenth

of our population goes to bed hungry, mostly children and the elderly.

Jesus shares his bread: "Take, eat. This is my body."

5. What can we do? Some fifth-grade pupils in California were asked by their teacher what they would do to reduce world hunger. "What can we do?" retorted one little boy, "We're not singers or pop stars."

But we *are* Christians with the Bread of Life!

6. Eating flesh. A few years ago, an airplane filled with people crashed on a peak in the Andes mountains. While waiting for rescue, some froze to death, while others were in danger of starving. The few survivors related how they were forced to eat the flesh of dead passengers in order to keep alive.

7. Left-over Communion Bread. In 1986, the World Methodist Church had a convention in Nairobi, Kenya. The Holy Communion was celebrated. Seventy loaves of bread were ordered for the service, but twenty-five consecrated loaves were not used. What to do with them? After the service, leaders gave the remaining bread to guards, security personnel, and to the homeless and hungry walking the streets in search of food. While giving the bread, a leader said, "This is the body of Christ, shared with you by Methodist friends from around the world."

8. What holy bread can do. The young associate pastor had recently been assigned to her first parish and was directed to visit a nursing home and administer the sacrament of Holy Communion to an elderly woman. Arriving at the nurses' station, she was told, "It's no use going to see her. She doesn't even recognize her children." Forewarned, she entered the room and found the woman gazing out the window, babbling incoherently. Deciding to do her duty, the pastor began from the Prayerbook and continued, though there seemed to be no comprehension on the part of the old woman. "What an exercise in futility," the young woman thought. And she wondered if anything at all was being heard. Only once did the drone of the elderly lady's voice change. As the elements of the Lord's Supper touched her mouth, she stopped making noises long enough to swallow them. The young pastor finished with the prayer of thanksgiving, and was readying herself to leave, when the old woman suddenly rolled over in bed, turned to her, and said, "God really does love us, doesn't he?" Something obviously had gotten through, triggering a memory planted long, long ago.

— Stephen C. Butler in *Pulpit Digest,* 10/86, p. 78.

Proper 28 • Pentecost 26 • Ordinary Time 33

Common   Lutheran   Roman Catholic

---

8. The Budding Fig Tree

Mark 13:24-32
Parallel: Luke 21:29-33 (Advent 1, C)

---

[24] *"But in those days, after that tribulation, the sun will be darkened, and the moon will not give its light,* [25] *and the stars will be falling from heaven, and the powers in the heavens will be shaken.* [26] *And then they will see the Son of man coming in clouds with great power and glory.* [27] *And then he will send out the angels, and gather his elect from the four winds, from the ends of the earth to the ends of heaven.*

[28] *"From the fig tree learn its lesson: as soon as its branch becomes tender and puts forth its leaves, you know that summer is near.* [29] *So also, when you see these things taking place, you know that he is near, at the very gates.* [30] *Truly, I say to you, this generation will not pass away before all these things take place.* [31] *Heaven and earth will pass away, but my words will not pass away.*

[32] *"But of that day or that hour no one knows, not even the angels in heaven, nor the Son, but only the Father."*

Are we able to read the signs of the times for what the future will bring? As a child I heard it said that a red sky in the morning meant a good day, but that a red sky in the evening warned of a coming storm.

If a groundhog in Pennsylvania sees his shadow, so the supersition goes, we can expect six more weeks of winter.

When we see squirrels gather nuts even in eighty-degree weather in the fall, we realize that winter is around the corner.

If nations spend billions of dollars to stockpile nuclear weapons, can we see that war is an approaching possibility?

In 1986, there was a nuclear disaster in Chernobyl, Russia. Over 100,000 people had to be evacuated in a nineteen mile danger zone and eighty people died from radiation sickness. Soviet physicians learned from Chernobyl that in the event of a nuclear war the medical system would be absolutely helpless. Is this nucler accident a portent of what would happen to the world if a nuclear outbreak occurred?

What about the end of the world and Christ's return? Is the end coming? If so, will it come soon? Jesus uses the same method as we do to tell what is coming when he gives the parable of the budding fig tree. Do you see the trees' tender branches and the leaves about to appear at springtime? Open your eyes! Can't you see that a new season is close at hand? Observe and learn! Look at the world condition: Does it not intimate that the end is coming and Christ is returning?

Context

Context of the Day

The parable of the budding fig tree is a part of the Gospel for the Twenty-Sixth Sunday after Pentecost (Proper 28). The parable harmonizes with the theme of the Sunday — the approaching end of the world and the return of Christ. The purpose of the parable is to alert us to the imminent Parousia.

Proper 28 (Pentecost 26) is the penultimate Sunday of the church year. The following Sunday is Christ the King Sunday, the end of the church year. Following Christ the King is the First Sunday in Advent, the beginning of a new church year. On the Lutheran calendar, the Day will only very rarely be observed because of the variable date of Easter, which falls on the first Sunday after the full moon, the vernal equinox. Easter comes between March 21 and April 25, and the church year adjusts to the date of Easter. An early Easter calls for a short Epiphany season and a long Pentecost season and, when Easter is late, the Epiphany season is long and the Pentecost season is short. Between 1987 and 2002, Easter comes only four times in March. This means that Pentecost 26 (Lutheran) may be used only four times in fifteen years. In the Common and Roman Catholic lectionaries, however, this Sunday is marked regularly.

If the Lutheran calendar drops out the parable of the budding fig tree close to the end of Cycle B, Lutherans will get to use it at the beginning of Cycle C.

Context of the Lectionary

The First Lesson. (Daniel 7:9-14) The last of the four beasts coming out of the sea was to be destroyed when the Ancient of Days (Yahweh) took his seat on the throne of judgment and gave to the Son of man (Christ) power, glory, and dominion with an everlasting Kingdom. At the judgment, the evil kingdoms of the world are destroyed and God's Kingdom is forever established.

The Second Lesson. (Hebrews 10:11-18) After offering himself on the Cross as the perfect sacrifice for sin, Christ ascended to the right hand of God and there waited for his enemies to be made the stool for his feet. As in the First Lesson, therefore, Christ is seen to return to the Father in victory and majesty where his enemies are subject to his rule.

Gospel. (Mark 13:24-32) When the universe collapses, Christ will return to Earth and gather his people from the ends of the Earth. As we may perceive by the coming of the leaves on the trees that summer is near, so we also know by the signs of the times that Jesus is coming soon. Though generations pass away and the cosmos crashes, Jesus' teachings are everlasting. Even though world conditions hint at the time of Jesus' return, no one — not even Jesus — knows the exact day or hour.

Context of the Propers

In harmony with the theme of the Lessons, the liturgical Propers deal with the end of time, the destruction of evil, and the victorious establishment of God's Kingdom. The Psalm of the Day (Psalm 145:8-13) proclaims "Thy kingdom is an everlasting kingdom."

In the Prayer of the Day we say, "always keeping in mind the end of all things and the day of judgment, we may be stirred up to holiness of life here and may live with you forever in the world to come."

The Hymn of the Day, "Through the Night of Doubt and Sorrow," portrays God's people on a pilgrimage from and through a world of doubt and sorrow to the promised land of eternal life in and with Christ.

Context of the Scriptures: Parallel Passages

Matthew 24:32-35. Matthew's account is almost identical in content to Mark's account of the impending end of the world and the Parousia. Matthew, however, also relates the experience of the people in Noah's day: While these people carried on their day-to-day activities, the flood came, and buried them — just as people who are unprepared and unaware of conditions today will be surprised when the end comes and Jesus returns.

Luke 21:29-33. According to Luke, Jesus refers not only to a fig tree but also to "all the trees." Tender branches and new leaves, after all, are not peculiar to a fig tree. Luke adds that when the universe falls apart at Jesus' return, we are to "look up and raise your heads, because your redemption is drawing near."

Various Fig Trees
1. The budding fig tree — Matthew 24:32-33; Mark 13:28-29; Luke 24:32-33.
2. The cursed fig tree — Matthew 21:18-22; Mark 11:12-14
3. The barren fig tree — Luke 13:6-9

The Fig Tree in Other Passages
Genesis 3:7 — Adam and Eve make aprons out of fig leaves.
1 Kings 4:25 — Sitting under one's fig tree is said to be a sign of prosperity and happiness.
2 Kings 20:7 — A cake of figs cures King Hezekiah's boil.
John 1:48 — Jesus sees Nathanael under a fig tree.
James 3:12 — A fig tree cannot yield olives.
Revelation 6:13 — The stars fall to earth as the fig tree sheds its winter fruit when shaken by a gale.

Content

Precis (Mark 13:24-32)

When the days of tribulation are over, the sun will not shine and the moon will not be seen. The stars will fall and the planets will leave their courses. Then Christ will be seen coming with great power and glory. He will gather his faithful people from the ends of the earth.

A fig tree can teach you a lesson. When the branches become tender and new leaves start coming, you know that summer is close. Similarly, when you see the tribulations you will know the time of Christ's coming is at hand. These tribulations will happen before those now living will die, but though heaven and earth disappear, Christ's words will not pass away. No one, however, not even the angels or God's Son, knows the day and the hour of the end except for God the Father.

Thesis: Current world conditions suggest the imminent return of Christ.

Theme: The telltale marks of Christ's return.

The Parable in the Gospel for Today

The parable of the budding fig tree should be seen, undestood, and used in preaching in relation not only to the gospel for today but also in light of the entire thirteenth chapter of Mark. The parable consists of two verses — the parable itself and one additional verse for Jesus' application. The parable by itself simply says that we know summer is just around the corner when a fig tree sends out its leaves. The parable, however, needs to be more deeply understood in the light of the world's end and Christ's return. As the leaves of the tree indicate approaching summer, so world conditions (destruction of the temple, wars, persecution of the faithful, false Christs) intimate that the end is near and that Christ is at the door of his return. In addition to the tree's revelation of the approaching Parousia, the Gospel also tells us the how, the when, and the purpose of his coming. It would therefore be inappropriate and improper to treat the parable independently of the last days.

Key Words in the Parable

1. "That tribulation." (v. 24) After "that tribulation" the universe will collapse and Christ will return. "That tribulation" will trigger the chaos to the end of the world. What tribulation is this?

In chapter 13 there are several tribulations mentioned, but probably "that" refers to the destruction of the temple. This would mark the end of the Jewish religion, the old covenant, and the beginning of the new covenant and Christianity as a universal religion. Many horrible things can happen — war, earthquake, famine, etc. — but the worst of these is the destruction of God's house because this symbolizes the obliteration of religious faith.

2. **"Shaken."** (v. 25) The heavens of the planets and the stars are to be "shaken", says the parable. Is this to be taken figuratively or literally? According to this passage, the sun's face will be hidden, and consequently the moon will not reflect the sun's light. In the aftermath of a nuclear holocaust the sun can literally be hidden by radioactive clouds and a nuclear winter result when the sun's rays cannot reach the earth. This would be the end of life on Earth, but whether the planet itself will be exploded into nothingness is still open to question.

3. **"Gather."** (v. 27) When Christ returns, he will send out his angels to the four corners of the Earth to gather to himself his faithful people. Until he comes, however, we experience the winter of his physical absence, but his coming brings to us the summer of his eternal presence. Because of this, God's people can rejoice, and they can look forward to the Parousia because then it will be summertime. No reference is made concerning those who do not belong to the "elect" — e.g., Mark makes no reference to a judgment when Christ comes. However, if the elect are gathered to Christ, the non-elect are apparently separated from Christ. And separation means death and hell.

4. **"These things."** (v. 29) When people see "these things," they will know Jesus is on the threshold of his return. What are "these things"? They refer to the cosmic collapse detailed in verses 1-23. In verse 7, the Disciples are told not to be alarmed when they hear of wars, because "these must take place, but the end is not yet." In the history of the world there have been many wars, earthquakes, famines, persecutions, and false prophets, yet the end has not come. The question remains: What set of tribulations will precede the cosmic end and the Parousia?

5. "Near." (v. 30) When the tree buds and leaves begin to form, we will know that Christ's time of coming is near and he is "at the very gates." That the end is near may be certain — but how near? To avoid unnecessary speculation, Jesus tells us that only the Father knows the precise time of the end. In Mark 13:10 Jesus said that "the gospel must first be preached to all nations" before the end will come. In his second letter, Peter explains the delay of Jesus' coming: "The Lord is not slow about his promise as some count slowness, but is forbearing toward you, not wishing that any should perish, but that all should reach repentance." (2 Peter 3:9) According to these statements, then, the Parousia may not be as near as we think; it will be a long time until all peoples of the world hear the gospel and all come to repentance.

6. "Generation." (v. 30) Jesus says that "this generation will not pass away before all these things take place." Some interpret this to mean that Christ was saying that he would come again before *his* generation passed, and that Jesus was apparently mistaken, therefore, about the time of his return. But this interpretation is itself mistaken since Jesus' words more clearly mean his generation would see the tribulations, such as the destruction of the temple, (13:1-23) come to pass.

7. "Pass away." (v. 31) This verse seems to be out of place in the present discussion of the Parousia. It is, however, quite appropriately placed when we view the context more carefully. Jesus had just spoken of the passing away of the heavens upon his return and also of a generation passing away. In the midst of this chaos and change, Jesus then assures us that his words are everlasting, and that he and his teachings are the point of stability in a changing world. Faced with these traumatic changes, we would otherwise be scared to death and utterly confused. The writer of Psalm 46 knew of these solid foundations: "Therefore will not we fear, though the earth be removed, and though the mountains be carried into the midst of the sea . . . Be still and know that I am God." The author of Hebrews urged his people to be grateful for "receiving a kingdom that cannot be shaken." (Hebrews 12:28)

Contemplation

Insights

1. Message of the parable and its context.

   A. A cosmic collapse will follow the tribulations listed in 13:1-23.

   B. At the time of the cosmic chaos, Christ will return in glory and power — v. 26.

   C. These troubled times (vv. 1-23) warn us that his coming is near — v. 29.

   D. Christ is coming to gather his people — v. 27.

   E. Though all things pass away, Christ's words are eternal — v. 30

   F. Though world conditions indicate that the end is near, no one but God knows the exact time of Christ's return and the world's end — v. 32.

2. Summer of salvation. "Summer is near" says Jesus in the parable. This summer represents warmth, longer days, and new growth in field and orchard, and it is the best time of the year. Winter means the opposite, and we are now in the wintertime because Christ is physically absent. But summer will be here when Christ returns to be with us always.

This concept changes our attitude toward the Parousia and the Day of the Lord. Many dread and fear the end and Christ's return, for they think of the Parousia only in terms of judgment and the prospect of hell. In Mark's account, however, there is no mention of judgment, and Christ simply returns to gather his faithful people. This means salvation, deliverance from an evil world, and the joy of fellowship with Christ. Christians can look forward with great anticipation to his coming and, indeed, even fervently pray for him to come quickly — "Maranatha!" This, therefore, does not eliminate the judgment altogether, however, for if only the "elect" are to be gathered, then where are the non-elect? But in Mark, the emphasis is upon the positive: the gathering of the faithful to be forever with the Lord.

3. Christ and Chaos: "When you see these things" (v. 29), "as soon as its branch becomes tender and puts forth its leaves . . ."

(v. 28) These things are the penultimate and the ultimate signs. Christ says he will return not at the penultimate signs but at the ultimate. The penultimate indications are described in 13:1-23 and consist of wars, earthquakes, famine, destruction of the temple, persecution of followers, and the coming of false prophets. Most people consider these as signs of the Parousia, but Jesus says, "No. When you hear of wars and rumors of wars do not be alarmed; this must take place, but the end is not yet." (v. 6) The penultimate signs warn us of the ultimate dissolution of the universe as described in vv. 24-25 and it is only that time that Christ is to return. Given our present nuclear capablity, we are quite clearly at the point of destroying the Earth, hiding the sun and moon with a nuclear cloud, and turning summer into a permanent winter. When this happens, Christ will come to deliver his people. In the midst of this cosmic chaos, the comforting aspect is to be found in the certainty of deliverance and in the eternal words of Christ — e.g., "my words shall not pass away." (v. 31)

Homily Hints

1. A Tree Speaks. (13:28) The parable of the budding fig tree speaks to us today about the end of the world and Christ's return. What does the tree say?

 A. Look at me — tender branch and coming leaves.

  Know what is going on in the world. Look at the conditions. It asks us to recognize our situation and predicament.

 B. Hear me — "know"

  Through the tree, God is saying something to us. We are to know and understand the meaning of the world situation and its relation to the Parousia.

2. Christ is Coming. (13:28-29) "Summer is near." The coming of Christ means the coming of summer for his people — the warmth of his presence, the harvest of his Kingdom. The parable and its context tells us the facts of his coming.

 A. Christ *is* coming again — v. 26

 B. How he is coming: with power and glory — v. 26

 C. Why he is coming: to gather the faithful — v. 27

 D. When he is coming: at an unexpected moment — v. 32

3. How Near is Near? (13:28-29) When the leaves start coming, summer is "near" and it means that Christ also is "near" — at the very gates. But how near is "near?" People have usually believed that the return of Christ would be in their own generation. Paul, for example, faced the problem that some of his people refused to work because they expected Jesus to come that very week! His coming may be farther away than we think, however. The end is not yet present because:

    A. The penultimate signs do not mean the end — 13:7
    B. The gospel must first be preached to all nations — 13:10
    C. All must come to repentance — 2 Peter 3:9

4. Living During End Times (13:24-31) We may be living in the end and yet not know it. Our text deals with these end times, and it tells us what we can expect before, during, and after the Parousia.

    A. Before the end: tribulations — v. 30
    B. At the end: chaos and Christ — vv. 24-27
    C. After the end: gathering with Christ, security — vv. 27, 31

Contact

Problems

1. Is Christ coming again or not? Before we can prepare a sermon on the parable of the budding fig tree, we must first know the answer to the above question. If Christ is not returning, there is no need for a sermon on this subject. On the other hand, however, some may believe that Christ already came when the Spirit came on Pentecost and that he is present in the church today. In this case also, a sermon on the parable is unnecessary.

According to a 1986 survey by the Princeton Religion Research Center, sixty-two percent of Americans belive Jesus will return some day. According to this poll, then, over one-third of Americans do not believe in the Parousia. If we preachers and Christians believe that Jesus will return, then we have a challenge to persuade all people to believe in his coming.

To preach on today's parable demands a belief in the Parousia. Why should we believe it? For one thing, the Bible teaches it: the subject of the Second Coming occurs 1,845 times in the Bible, 318 times in the New Testament; seven out of every ten chapters in the

New Testament refer to the Parousia. Moreover, the church has believed in it since the first century, for Sunday after Sunday she confesses in the Apostles' Creed: "From thence he shall come to judge the living and the dead."

2. Is the Second Coming to be taken seriously? Is it possible that church people no longer take the Parousia seriously? In some denominations, the sermon refers to it almost every Sunday, and Gospel hymns and anthems are often also on the subject. Is it possible we could be "crying wolf" so often that we are no longer being heard? The church year and lectionary call upon us to deal with the subject at the end and the beginning of the church year. We hear the same passage at least once a year, year after year. But since the first century each generation has believed Christ would come in that generation. If time after time he did not come, why would anyone be concerned about his coming in our generation?

This is a real problem for the preacher. The fact is that there is always the possibility that today is the day of his return. No one knows the time, and we must live constantly with the possibility. This calls for living each day in a state of grace in the event that Christ should come today or tomorrow.

3. Interpretation. The parable of the budding fig tree is subject to faulty interpretation. From one viewpoint, the budding tree is supposed to represent the nation of Israel founded in 1948. In addition, this view claims that the Parousia will occur during the generation following 1948. Evidently, this is a case of allegorization and eisegesis by those who see modern Israel as a sign of the end of time. This interpretation is plainly an abuse of the Bible and cannot be supported by biblical scholarship.

4. Limitations. The Gospel containing the parable has two limitations in developing a full understanding of the Parousia. First, the pericope does not give us any practical follow-up of the Second Coming. We are told to read the signs of the times, to know the cosmic collapse when Jesus returns, to be sure that Jesus' words are eternal, and to be uncertain about the day of his return but so what? What are the moral implications of this knowledge? Is there anything we need to do about it? If we need such practical application, we will have to go to Luke's account of the parable which comes on the first Sunday in Advent, Series C. Luke adds, for example, "Take heed to yourselves . . . " (Luke 21:34)

The other limitation is in today's pericope that Mark gives no account of the judgment that is to occur when Christ returns. According to Mark, Jesus comes back at the end of time to gather his "elect," but there is no mention of the separation of sheep and the goats and no sending of the wicked to hell. The emphasis in Mark's account is positive, and it is a time of reunion with Christ, salvation, and heaven. But this is only one side of the coin. For the other side, we must go to another evangelist.

Point of Contact

1. **Controversy.** The Second Coming is a live subject among church people today. In verse 32 Jesus plainly said that only the Father knows the day of the end and the return of Christ. In spite of this, some groups of Christians seem to know more than Jesus or the angels on this matter. In the 15th century the Taborites, for instance, fixed the date in the middle of February. The Seventh Day Adventist claimed the end would come on October 22, 1844. Jehovah's Witnesses and the Mormons also set a date. In more recent times, Fundamentalist leaders use the books of Daniel and Revelation to determine a specific date. In response, the Lutheran Council in the United States prepared a statement in 1986 which opposed this date fixing. The statement objects to the view that current history is in a countdown stage toward the imminent end. The paper declared, "To make human measurements out of heavenly visions is simply a forced imposition on the text."

2. **Popularity.** The Second Coming is a popular subject in contemporary society. Many are fascinated by the prospect of the world's destruction. When will it all end? How will it end? We are a society faced with star wars, nuclear war, violence, and terrorism. When the world appears to be hopeless and people are desperate, they become interested in last things.

It is a popular subject with Fundamentalists, Pentecostals, and Charismatics. It is often the main theme of sermons and songs. The lack of attention given to the Parousia by mainline churches gives the impression that they do not believe in it. But they *do* believe in the Parousia and each year it is the subject for consideration according to the church calendar and lectionary. But, the doctrine needs to be kept in proper perspective with the total Gospel.

3. Ultimate Questions. People in the pews are asking ultimate questions about life and the world. They hear various answers which conflict with each other. They want clear and true answers to questions like these: Whose world is this — God's or Satan's? Will God allow humanity to destroy his world? In the event of a nuclear holocaust, will there be any people on Earth when Christ returns? Will wrongs be righted and justice be meted out to those who committed crimes and got away with them on Earth? Does history go on endlessly without meaning or consummation? Is it possible that God will use a nuclear destruction as the scene for Jesus' return? All of these questions — and more — are involved in preaching on the parable of the budding fig tree.

Illustrative Materials

Awareness
"Earth's crammed with heaven,
And every common bush afire with God;
But only he who sees, takes off his shoes —
The rest sit round it and pluck blackberries,
And daub their natural faces unaware
More and more from the first similitude!"

— Browning

Some years ago, a botanist was studying the heather bell on the highlands of Scotland. While he was studying the flower, a shepherd came up to him and asked what he was doing. Rather than try to explain, he invited the shepherd to look at a flower through his microscope. When the shepherd saw the glorious beauty of the flower, he explained, "My God, and I have been trampling on them all my life!"

The End?
In 1986 a United Nations expert predicted that an all-out nuclear war would kill about four billion people, 4/5ths of the world population. If the entire world's nuclear arsenal, equivalent to thirty

billion tons of TNT were used, one billion people in the northern hemisphere would be killed.

The Academy of Atomic Scientists has a doomsday clock. The Scientists see the end of the world at the time of a nuclear war. At the resumption of the cold war and Russia's invasion of Afghanistan, the scientists moved the clock up to seven minutes before midnight.

H. G. Wells: "The world is at the end of its rope. The end of everything we call life is close at hand."

Albert Einstein: "The ghost-like character of this development lies in its apparently compulsory trend. In the end there beckons more and more clearly general annihilation."

Allan Munn, Canadian physicist: The thermonuclear devices now with us "might cause the world and all in it to disintegrate in less than a minute."

Time of Coming

In *Fiddler on the Roof* a young Jew implores, "Rabbi, we've been waiting for the Messiah all our lives. Wouldn't this be a good time for him to come?"

A celebrated American novelist tells of a time in his youth when for several years he was a street preacher of hellfire and damnation. Once he told his listeners that the world would come to an end the following Saturday. A cynic later asked him, "What did you tell them the following Sunday when the end had not come to pass?" "Why," he said, "I told them that the world had been miraculously saved by our prayers."

Anticipation

A preacher was describing the end of the world. "Lightning will crackle," he said, "thunder will boom, rivers will overflow, flames will shoot down from the heavens, and darkness will fall over the world." A small boy turned to his father and asked, "Do you think they will let school out early?"

About the Author

John R. Brokhoff was born in Pottsville, Pennsylvania. After graduation from high school, he attended Muhlenberg College in Allentown, Pennsylvania. Upon graduating, Brokhoff attended Philadelphia Lutheran Seminary from which he was ordained. He later received his Masters degree from the University of Pennsylvania and his Doctor of Divinity degree from Muhlenberg College.

Dr. Brokhoff is married to the former Barbara McFarland, who also is an ordained minister in the Methodist church, and is an evangelist for the Florida Conference. Dr. Brokhoff and his wife are a teacher/preacher team who are in demand across the country for conferences and conventions.

Dr. Brokhoff served parishes in Pennsylvania, North Carolina, Georgia, and Virginia. He is also professor emeritus of homiletics at Candler School of Theology, Emory University. Throughout over thirty years in the active ministry, Dr. Brokhoff has also found the time to be a prolific author — with fifteen books in print and two more being published at the time this volume goes to press.